Marketing for the Slightly Uncertain

Fiona Stuart-Wilson MA(Cantab), Assoc. IPD, MIMC CMC
and
Mike Grace BDS, DGDP (UK)

2000

Published by the British Dental Association
64 Wimpole Street, London W1M 8AL

ISBN 0 904588 62 9

Printed and bound by
Dennis Barber Graphics and Print, Lowestoft, Suffolk

Foreword

During the 1990s dentistry, like many other professions, experienced major and rapid changes in its approach to the business aspects of running a professional practice. Perhaps the most important change is the necessity for healthcare professionals to appreciate that the business needs of a practice or organisation should not be considered as a necessary (and unwanted) set of activities that must be added to the really important clinical activities. For real progress to be made dentists need to understand that patient care requires an integrated approach to both clinical and business requirements. The two work hand-in-hand.

Perhaps this way of thinking is best explored in the marketing approach to patient care. Although marketing has come a long way since the mid-1980s (when it was almost considered to be a necessary evil foisted on the profession) the concept of marketing is still misunderstood. This book will demonstrate how a marketing approach to patient care can be integrated into all other management aspects of running a successful dental practice, whether in general practice, the community or the hospital environment.

The essence of marketing is that it is a process that continues all the time, and that it balances the requirements of the customer (patient) with the objectives and operating environment of the business. Marketing should not be biased one way or the other if the business is to succeed. Thus a marketing approach does not state that the customer is always right to the exclusion of everything else, especially the professional guidance the dentist provides. By the same token, marketing recognises that effective progress is more likely when the patient's needs and wants play a large part in the development of practice strategy and activities. It is much easier to help people buy your services when those services provide your customers with something they appreciate and want.

Perhaps one of the biggest difficulties for dentists in understanding marketing is the plethora of models, acronyms and jargon surrounding the subject, most of which appear to have no relevance to dental practice. We have tried to demystify these models as much as possible, at the same time introducing a new model we feel is more appropriate to dentistry. The difficulty is that the existing marketing concepts and tools tend to exist without a clear overall model to fit them all into, introducing potential confusion. In essence, marketing can be a difficult thing to understand at first.

This is why we have tried to create an operating model that enables you to get started without necessarily understanding everything there is to know. As you progress around the cycle of our operating model you will begin to see how all the different aspects of marketing work with each other. Often though, understanding comes more from doing than from knowing when you are embarking on your marketing plan.

Our aim in this book is to make marketing simpler, easier and more understandable so that dentists and their staff can start to make marketing work in their organisations. For many there is uncertainty at first (hence the title of the book) but for most a gradual immersion in the process starts to open doors of understanding which all begin to link together as you go on.

Marketing is one of the most exciting ways of gaining control over your business development, satisfying your customers and making money. It really does put you 'in the driving seat' so you can aim for the ideal situation of doing the dentistry you want to on the patients you want to and making the profit you want to. It isn't guaranteed (because virtually nothing in life is) but it is definitely more likely.

We wish you luck.

Contents

1 Is marketing for everyone?

Before we start looking at the marketing process we need to correct a few myths and misconceptions about marketing that we regrettably still see, often reinforced by marketing consultants.

In this first chapter we have detailed the myths we feel to be both most common and most inaccurate. It is helpful to consider what marketing is not, because a complete and correct understanding about what marketing is not will help you appreciate how marketing can benefit you and your practice or organisation, and how you need to integrate marketing into your management and clinical practice.

The myths of marketing

Myth 1: Marketing isn't professional

For some people the idea of using commercial principles in their professional life is difficult. Some healthcare professionals still believe that healthcare and business should not mix. While everyone is entitled to his own view, we believe that you not only can integrate commercial principles into professional care, but that you should. As we will show throughout this book, a professional practice (including hospital and community care) will improve its service for patients if it uses appropriate commercial principles in its daily activities.

Myth 2: Marketing isn't ethical

This myth is really a refinement of Myth 1. Some dentists appear to think that some business activities are appropriate for a dental practice, but that the process of marketing itself is not ethical. We suspect this is because the concept of marketing is poorly understood, and these dentists believe that marketing is a method of persuading people to buy something they do not need or want.

Obviously, persuading people to buy something they do not need is unethical, but this is not what marketing is about. We believe that marketing is essentially ethical as it enables informed patient choice and decision-making by the patient in partnership with the dentist.

Myth 3: Marketing is simply for those converting to private practice
Some people assume that marketing is used for converting your practice to private dentistry. While a thorough knowledge of marketing is essential to convert to a different system of payment for your patients, marketing is required for all practices, for example both NHS and private in the UK, if they wish to reach their potential and get the most from professional practice.

Myth 4: Marketing is just advertising
Another misconception is that marketing means producing a practice brochure or putting an advertisement in the local telephone directory. Brochures and advertisements are part of marketing, but only a small part of the process.

Promoting your practice, be it through brochures, advertisements or other means, must be part of the whole marketing package. The danger of promotional activity (such as producing a brochure) before you have carried out some market research or identifed your marketing objectives is you will probably be making a very expensive mistake by trying to communicate inappropriate messages to the wrong people.

Myth 5: Marketing means getting more patients
Many people equate marketing with increasing the patient base, and as many dental organisations have more than enough patients already they tend to disregard marketing altogether. This means they lose the opportunities that a market-led approach would offer them, including doing the kind of dentistry they prefer, attracting the kind of patients who require the kind of treatment they would prefer to offer, and improving job satisfaction for the whole team.

Myth 6: Marketing is another name for selling
The concept of selling has now entered the dental vocabulary, and not before time. Regrettably, selling is often equated with marketing, and many people get the two confused. Marketing is the whole process of finding out what customers want, anticipating future trends in the market, producing an appropriate service to satisfy the requirements of the people in your chosen market, attracting them to you and only then selling to them. Selling is the transaction that occurs at the point of contact when the patient is deciding

whether to accept the treatment plan offered or dental services.

Myth 7: Marketing is all about persuasion
Another common misconception is that marketing is really about persuading people to buy your products or services (often against their better judgement). While some companies and people do try to use marketing techniques to achieve this, it is not only unethical but also unnecessary. Effective (and ethical) marketing is about the balance between providing people with what they want and developing the appropriate service for you to offer, not persuading them to desire what you want to sell to them.

Myth 8: Marketing does not involve the whole practice
In many organisations, including single-handed general dental practice, people suffer from the misconception that marketing is only for the owner or the senior management, or marketing department. Marketing is much more effective if everyone in the organisation realises that all members of the practice, especially the receptionists and dental nurses, require an understanding of marketing as well. This enables a fully-integrated approach to operate within the practice providing a much higher level of care for the patients because the whole team is contributing to both the creation and application of whole patient care.

Having looked at a few misconceptions, we now need to consider the benefits to the dental organisation of a marketing approach. We can consider this from the viewpoint of the dental practice and the patients.

What marketing does for the dental practice

Ideal dentistry on ideal patients

Two of the least understood benefits of marketing to the dentist is that it is both a way of helping attract the kind of patients you want to treat, and a way of carrying out the kind of dentistry you want to do more successfully.

This applies to all types of practice, whether government funded, insurance-funded or private practice. Dentists often seem to feel that they should open their doors to patients and accept all-comers. They can cope with the concept of specialist practice (in other words restricting patients by clinical need or want) but find it more difficult to cope with the concept of attracting types of patients, such as enthusiastic patients within a certain income group.

We are not suggesting that people should do this – simply that they can.

More profitability

Businesses operate on profit in most countries, and even government-funded operations (such as hospital trusts and community clinics) have to show a greater degree of accountability and value for money these days when compared with less than a decade ago. Thus making a profit, both in financial and health terms, is part of the requirements for success.

Marketing improves your chances of being more profitable, as it attracts those people who want what you have to offer. Part of this process involves pricing, as a more effective pricing policy is one way of increasing profits.

Better staff motivation

It seems evident that people tend to become more motivated and committed when practice goals are clear and the practice is doing the business it wants to. Obviously there is more to motivation than this, but supplying services to people who want and value them tends to be far more satisfying for everyone in the practice. It also tends to mean less stress for everyone, as priorities are clear and the practice is more focused.

What marketing does for the patients

Customer care

Probably the most important benefit that patients will perceive is that proper marketing tends to focus the practice on developing an appropriate level of customer care. This means that the practice considers all aspects of the patient's visit, whether clinical or non-clinical, and whether it meets patient requirements.

Listened to

It is crucial that marketing involves market research, or identifying and anticipating patient requirements. This means a constant and consistent approach to getting feedback from patients of their perception of the service. It is important to remember that to fulfil the ideal 'wants' of patients there must be an appropriate balance between the clinical requirements identified by the professional(in other words, what is wrong and how to treat it) and the desires of the patient.

The patient's desires are usually the same when it comes to clinical advice, but may be different in their objectives for oral health. For example, a patient may attend claiming that they 'want' to have all their teeth extracted and a set of complete dentures fitted. Obviously, this is not always an ideal solution, and the dentist needs to ask appropriate questions and listen to the patient to identify what he really wants. In this example, the patient really wants what he thinks having their teeth removed will produce, not the act of extraction itself. Once this has been identified the professional may be able to suggest alternative ways of achieving what the patient wants.

The essence of marketing

The Chartered Institute of Marketing defines marketing as:

> 'The management process involved in identifying, anticipating and satisfying customer requirements profitably'.

This definition is now used widely in many articles and books on marketing, and with good reason. It is a superb example of brevity and simplicity, yet every word in the definition is vital to a full understanding of the process. We need to examine these words carefully, as all of them have a direct part to play in an understanding of marketing continually.

Management

By itself this is another word that needs defining. If we use the concept that management is achieving things through people, then we appreciate the importance of the whole dental practice getting involved in marketing.

Process

Marketing is a process, not a 'one-off' event. Ensuring that the whole dental team commit to this concept is necessary if marketing is to be successful. It is not something that you just 'do' now and then, it is your whole approach to everything you do all the time.

Identifying

Marketing requires that you find out what your customers really want rather than assuming you know (or assuming that what you would want is what others would want).

Anticipating

Marketing means you need to try and estimate what customers are likely to want, or be interested in, in the future. This can obviously be checked by market research later.

Satisfying

Marketing involves giving people what they actually want in ways that meet or exceed their expectations (with the emphasis on 'their').

Customer

Marketing is always customer-focused. At times people lose sight of who their customers are. In simplistic terms it means the people paying the bill, but in actual terms customers are also people receiving the service you provide whether they pay you directly or not. Most businesses have several different types of customers, and all require an individual and appropriate marketing approach.

Requirements

The actual needs and wants of customers. The difference between the two is explained below.

Profitably

This can be the part people leave out of the equation, or forget to check. Marketing means making sure that what you provide meets the needs and wants of those who might buy it, while ensuring you still make a profit.

If people are only prepared to buy your services at a price that does not allow the business to make a profit then you either 'market' yourself better, or change what you are providing, or where you provide it.

A question of balance

One thing to remember is that 'customer-focused' does not mean having to do everything entirely for customers. The business is your business, one that you have chosen. Therefore, you must feel fullfilled in providing the services (unless you are purely money-motivated) and must be able to balance your own needs and requirements with those of your customers (and staff).

Marketing means taking the requirements of customers into account in the way you run the business and sell the services/products, rather than attempting to persuade people to buy simply because they ought to (a common belief among health workers) or because you want them to.

Although the definition from the Chartered Institute of Marketing is a good one, it omits the requirements of the business itself, or in our case the dentist. For this reason we would like to suggest another definition which restores the balance:

'Marketing is the art of balancing your objectives with the reality of the operating environment.'

This definition does not really tell us much about how to 'market', but it does focus on the need to try and balance what you want to sell with what people want to buy. A marketing approach should enable you to feel more confident that what you want to provide in terms of services and products will satisfy customer requirements. That is the ideal.

A marketing approach

A true marketing approach will include the following:

- Finding out what your customers want now (market research)
- Developing appropriate services
- Communicating with your target audiences about your services
- Selling the services to people you attract
- Gaining feedback about the services
- Ensuring the whole operation is profitable.

This is the basic marketing process. We can add levels of sophistication into this formula if we wish, as below:

- Finding out what your customers want now (market research)
- Anticipating what will interest your customers in the future
- Setting your marketing objectives in line with your business strategy
- Developing new, appropriate and innovative services
- Segmenting your market
- Promoting your products and services to your target audiences
- Selling the products and services to people you attract
- Ensuring the whole operation is profitable.

How people get it wrong

Many businesses get the marketing concept wrong, because they take the approach shown in Figure 1.1. People have what they think is a valuable service or product, and because they think it is wonderful, they assume others will too — and will thus buy it. Life does not work that way.

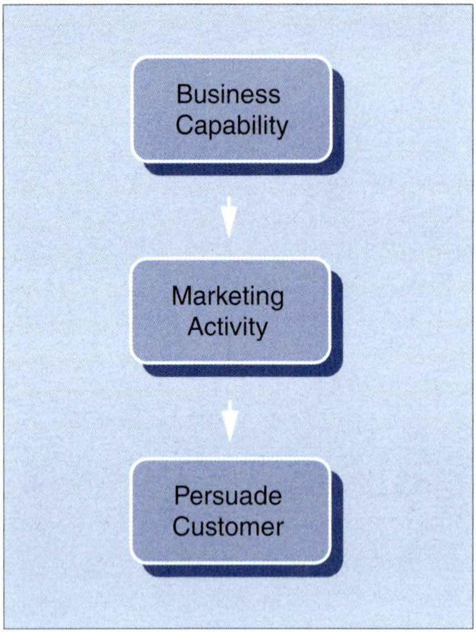

Fig.1.1 The wrong approach to marketing

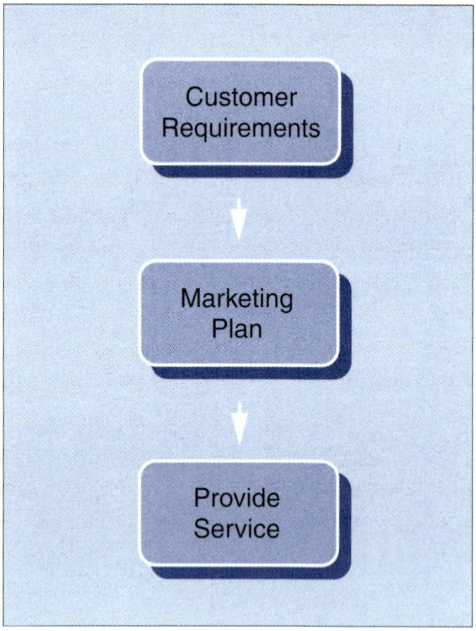

Fig.1.2 Getting the balance right

The marketing approach is to put the requirements of the customer first, develop the service based on a balance between the customer's requirements and the qualities and abilities of the business (Figure 1.2).The difficulty in business is that it is much easier to run the business in the way that the owner wants to. It is easier to design the recall system, provide appointment times, sort out the administration, arrange the layout and design of the surgery to suit the owner rather than the customer.While you must take your own wishes into account (after all, you work there all the time) you also need to find out what the patients would like and take them into account if you wish to retain your competitive edge. Remember that patients may flock through the door, but they can leave through it, too.

Marketing is just as much about retaining patients as recruiting new ones.

The difference between 'need' and 'want'

People get confused about the difference between need and want. We all have certain needs, and these can be simply defined using a model described by

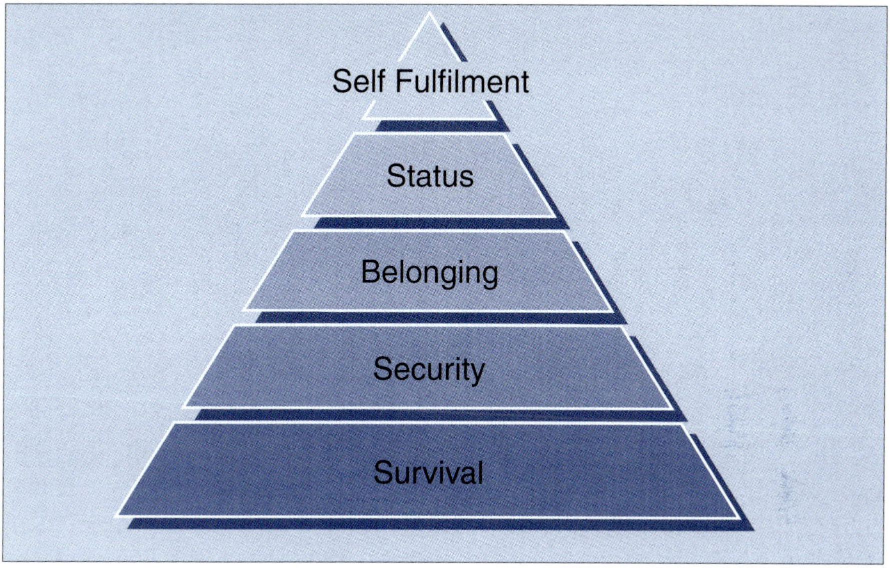

Fig.1.3 Maslow's Hierarchy of Needs

Abraham Maslow.

Maslow stated that people have certain basic needs. We start with a need for survival. Once this is satisfied, we need security. Again, once survival and security are satisfied we need to feel part of a social group, to belong. The next level is a need for status, and finally, once all other needs are satisfied, we feel a need for self-fulfilment. Maslow used a pyramid called the 'Hierarchy of Needs' for his model (Figure 1.3). This is a convenient way to think of our needs as many more people operate on the lower levels (security and survival). The difference between our wants and needs is that our 'wants' are the ways we choose to satisfy our needs. In simple terms, I must satisfy my survival need for food. I want to eat a sandwich, but I could have wanted to eat a pizza or have a meal at an expensive restaurant. The need does not change, but how I choose to satisfy that need does. My need for security might be to have a job, but while some people want an employed position (because they see it as more secure than running their own business) others will perceive owning a business as more secure than a job from which they can be dismissed or made redundant.

The status level perhaps shows the differences between need and want

The basic marketing questions

1. What business you are in?
2. What is your product or service?
3. Who are your customers?
4. What is your marketing plan?

Fig.1.4 The four main aspects of marketing

more easily. We all have a need for status but we all tend to satisfy it in different ways. For some, designer clothes satisfy that need. For some the make and model model of our car is our status 'fix'. For others, jewellery will provide status, whilst still others will use work (or their position) to satisfy the need. Work can also be used to satisfy the need. We all 'buy' different services and products to satisfy our need. The need may be the same, but our wants definitely differ.

Aspects of marketing

There are four main aspects of marketing which are relevant to all small businesses, irrespective of the type of business (Figure 1.4). Every aspect of marketing should help to find out what customers want, how to meet their needs, and how to do so at a profit.

While some of these may seem simplistic and obvious, many businesses carry on operating making basic assumptions about all of these aspects. When the environment changes they can be caught out and find themselves doing the wrong things, at the wrong time (and often for the wrong reason). We will be considering these four aspects and the way they interact with each other, in more detail later. We will also be looking at a practical model called the Marketing Cycle (Figure 1.5) and explaining how this integrates with the other models we will be describing as we move through the whole process.

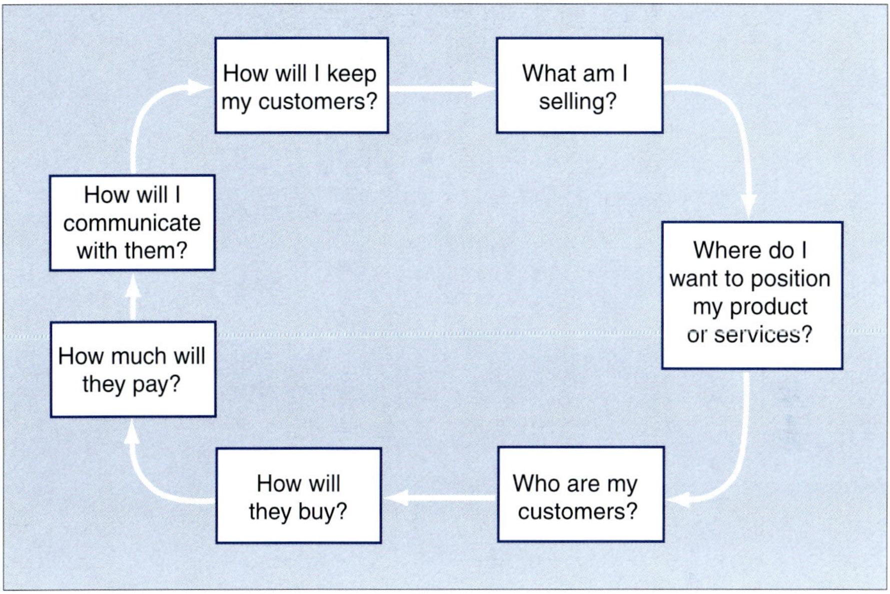

Fig.1.5 The marketing cycle

What business am I in?

2

This chapter is all about deciding what your practice or organisation is doing in terms that will make sense to its customers. In other words, it is answering the basic question — what business am I in?

Before we consider this question we need to look at the Marketing Cycle. Marketing can be viewed as a number of different models which both help explain how marketing works and, more importantly, how people can market their businesses successfully. Our model (Figure 2.1) will form a framework throughout the book, and will integrate with a number of other models as we progress round the cycle.

As you can see from Figure 2.1 we are entering the cycle at the stage of asking the question 'What am I selling?'. In terms of the balance mentioned in Chapter 1 between the objectives of the business and the requirements of potential customers this is where we have to start.

From an operating point of view the business is probably selling something already, and, if we need to get involved in some fairly rapid marketing activity, it seems sensible to continue with our existing products and services for the immediate future. But marketing really involves taking a step back to consider what business we are in. We may be missing out on potential new directions if we limit ourselves simply to our current services.

A few basics

At first sight the business you are in seems obvious. In fact, the question itself may seem an odd question. Surely, every business person knows what business he or she is in?

The conventional answers to this question tend to define the business in terms of its technology, products or services. For example dentists are in the business of dentistry (are they not?). Radio stations are in the business of broadcasting, and publishers are in the business of publishing.

A better answer is to look at the business from the viewpoint of the customer. Many companies find that when they focus on the customer to identify their

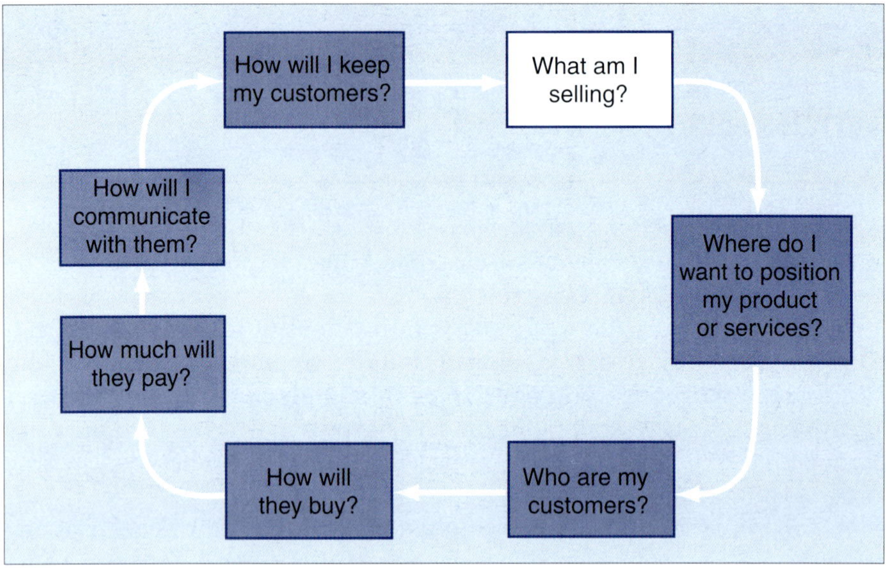

Fig.2.1 The marketing cycle: what am I selling?

business they broaden their scope of services and products. For example a firm of roofing contractors is in the business of supplying services to the building trade, not just supplying roofs. A railway provider is in the business of supplying transport, not trains.

An analogy in dentistry is obvious. Most dental practices think they are providers of dentistry. The focus of the practice is on teeth, the identification of dental problems and the provision of advice and treatment. In recent years this approach was widened to include prevention and cosmetic dentistry but the main emphasis still concentrated on providing treatment of some kind.

From the customer's viewpoint a dental practice is providing oral care, not just dental treatment. Patients see the dental treatment as only part of the process. This provides a wider vision that dental practices are in the healthcare market (with an emphasis on oral health care). Thus, from the clinical aspects of health care we can also consider mouth odour prevention and anti-smoking advice as being within the remit of our business.

However, important as the patient is, we must remember that the dentists themselves and the dental staff also have a major stake in the business. They

A dental example demonstrating the difference between strategy and tactics

It can be difficult to remember the difference between strategy and tactics, especially when confronted by the hectic whirl of dental practice.

One way of thinking of it that is more natural in dentistry is to remember the principles of treatment planning. When seeing a patient for an examination most dentists will consider principles first (eliminate pain, control caries, restore periodontal health, restore function, etc.) before deciding how to deal with the broken amalgam in the upper left premolar or the symptomless root retained in the mandible.

Considering the principles is the strategic approach. How to restore the broken amalgam or what to do with the retained root are the tactics – and how you treat the amalgam (crown, replacement, alternative material) or the retained root (extraction, leave post crown) should fit into the overall strategy for the mouth. The treatment will be different depending on the overall strategy for the mouth. The treatment will be different depending on the overall strategy you and the patient choose.

Fig.2.2 Strategy and tactics

need to be considered as part of the equation, so that the business caters for both the owners and staff as well as the customers. For this reason a good understanding of strategic planning and management is necessary to identify the business you are in and the direction you need to go, to maintain the balance between satisfying patients and providers.

Strategic planning

Planning involves thinking how to manage aspects of the business. Strategic planning looks at the broad methods of getting where you want to go. Tactical planning involves the day-to-day activities that help you achieve those broad aims.

People often confuse the terms strategy and tactics, both in theory and in practice. We tend to get caught up in what we need to do today, often reacting to events and people around us, rather than checking to see if we are still on track to meet our overall objectives and if the things that we are doing are really relevant. Strategy is the overall long-term plan. Tactics are the order and arrangement of tasks to achieve objectives along the way. Figure 2.2 illustrates a dental example of the difference.

Returning to the business side of things, your strategic objective may be to convert your practice to a specialist restorative practice, with 60% of turnover resulting from private patient treatment by December 31.

Some of the tactics you might employ to achieve this could include:

- Attending a course to keep up to date clinically
- Working out a price list
- Producing a brochure
- Analysing current financial information
- Training staff in ethical sales techniques.

None of these are strategic activities, but all of them should fit into your strategy. Obviously, the strategic thinking must come first, because otherwise you may be doing things that have no relationship to your overall direction.

A model for overall strategic planning

Figure 2.3 is a suggested model for helping put strategic planning into perspective — a logical and effective method of taking control of business planning.

This model shows how both strategy and tactics fit into an overall plan and starts with a purpose or mission statement. The term 'mission statement' is now accepted in most areas of business, so we will use it here. You have to know your overall reason for being in business and your main aim for the business. From this everything else should follow.

The broad plan for achieving your aims in business is your strategy. Following this you need strategic objectives which lead to tactics, or the tasks required (what you do on a day-to-day basis). Success indicators are the ways you tell if it is working.

Mission statement

The phrase 'mission statement' can be uncomfortable for many people. In simple terms, your mission statement is a statement of aims or purpose which succinctly tells everyone working in the organisation why they are there and what they are trying to do.

Surprisingly, staff in many organisations do not have a clear idea as to the purpose and the direction of the business. The people at the top of the organisation assume others know, the people working lower down don't care — the result is ineffective work, lack of motivation, lack of direction and lack

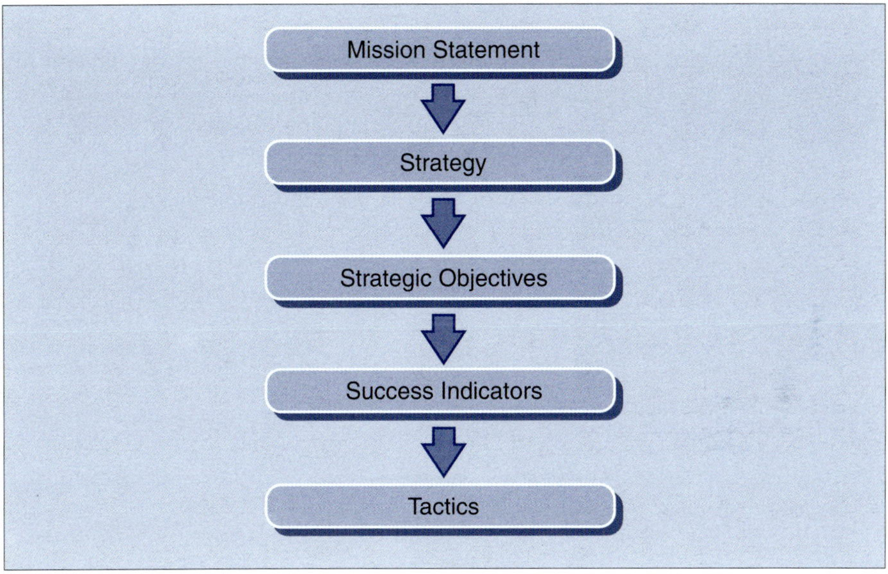

Fig.2.3 Strategic planning

of progress.

The other problem with mission statements is that often people can make them too complex (to try and incorporate all views and to protect against failure) so that no-one can remember them.

Mission statements should have:

- Vision — a worthwhile picture of where the business is going and why it is worth trying to get there
- Value — it must be important to everyone in the organisation and ideally important to the world at large. We all like to feel what we are doing is worthwhile
- Viability — it must be attainable even if never achieved. If achieved, set a new mission statement.

Strategy

Your strategy is the broad plan of achieving your mission statement. For convenience strategic management can be divided into five areas (Figure 2.4).

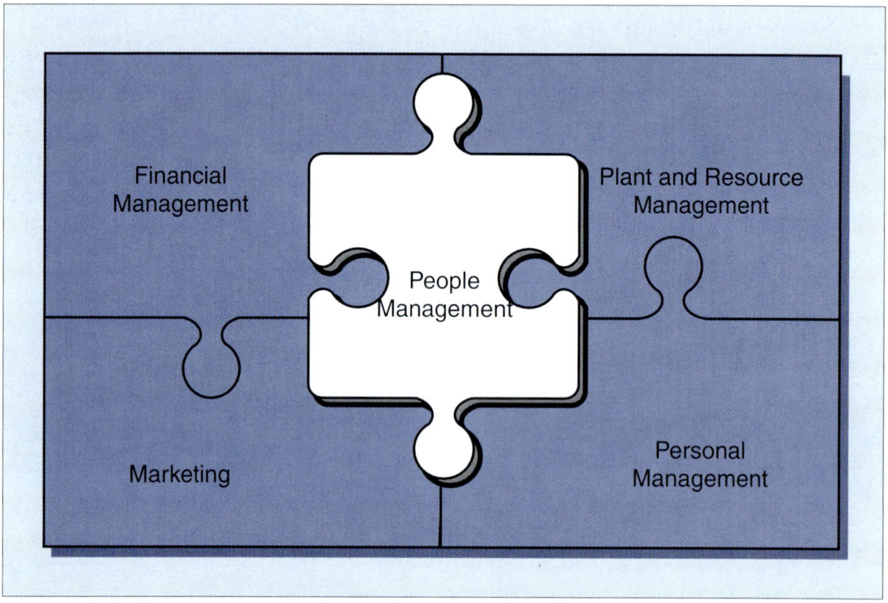

Fig.2.4 The Management Jigsaw

All these aspects of strategic management are important, and all of them tend to influence each other. For this reason we often think of them as pieces in a jigsaw puzzle. The financial aspects affect people management — how profitable the business is will be influenced by what the staff do — and equipment and resource management — can we afford to put in a new computer system? As owner, the dentist's personal management (his skills and training programme) obviously affects his ability to manage people, provide good customer care and look after the finances.

This is just one model of management and there are as many models as there are people to think them up. There is no 'right' model, simply different ways of looking at things.

We consider the above to be an easy one to remember, and a relevant one for dental practice. Note that managing people is the central piece of the jigsaw, the key to the whole thing.

Because marketing is closely integrated into the other aspects of strategic management we ought to consider the five aspects of management in a little more detail.

Financial management

Financial management means more than just watching the accountant do the accounts and pretending to understand the balance sheet at the annual meeting. The owner is responsible for the financial management of his business. While this does not require the owner to be an accountant, it does, however, require an understanding of what an accountant does and being able to provide a description of the businesses financial objectives.

A basic understanding includes the following:

- What a balance sheet and profit and loss account are for, and how to read both
- How to carry out a cash flow forecast
- What depreciation is and what it means
- The significance of working capital
- Basic principles of personal financial protection
- How to keep simple book keeping accounts (manual or computerised)
- How to set and monitor budgets.

Financial management is essential in strategic planning, and links to both pricing and profit in your marketing strategy.

Plant and resource management

This aspect of management involves managing equipment, property, leases, etc. Health and safety aspects can come under this heading, as do radiological guidelines and cross infection control. For the purposes of most practices a good system and appropriate training are the keys to successful management.

Marketing

Marketing means considering patient recruitment, retention and non-clinical management of patients (sometimes referred to as customer care) as well as the more traditional aspects of marketing such as promotion and market research. All this has to be balanced with an ethical requirement to provide quality clinical care and to restore patients to good oral health.

Personal management

This area is one of the most neglected in all strategic management — looking after your own personal development. People will often assume that they can continue to develop their business and their ability to manage it without considering their own development, their own need to build skills in organisation, time management, stress management, decision-making and leadership.

Unless managers continue their own development they will create stress by raising their expectations of performance without the backup of increased knowledge and skills.

People management

People are the strongest (and the weakest) link in strategic management because they are so unpredictable. The management of people is the central link to all the other areas and impinges on all the other areas as well.

People management involves an understanding of behaviour and how to respond to and influence it. We cannot tell people what to think (nor should we) but we can tell them what we would like them to do and how we would like them to behave, and expect them to accept this and do it.

In marketing terms people management applies to both the management of staff and patients.

Strategic objectives

These are the steps you need to take to achieve your strategic aims. Every business looks at objectives as a means of achieving its goals and controlling its direction.

However, objectives can be difficult to set, partly because people are not always sure of the overall direction of the business and partly because objectives need to be clear and very specific if they are to be achieved. People tend not to be very specific because it is easier to think in general terms. People often claim that their objective is 'to improve communication' but never clarify what they mean by this. To take this objective to extremes, we could say that for the dentist to say 'good morning' to the staff every day instead of four days out of five is an improvement in communication.

The danger with a non-specific objective is that no-one really knows what they need to do (the tactics) to achieve it and so nothing gets done. The objective is always 'something we must get around to' rather than something we are actively addressing.

SMART Objectives

To be effective objectives must fulfil certain criteria, often referred to by the acronym SMART (Figure 2.5).

Specific
Measurable
Achievable
Realistic
Time-bound

Fig.2.5 SMART objectives

Analysing how SMART an objective is

Example:
Our objective is to become more profitable

This raises a number of questions:

- How much more profitable? 1%? 20%? 50%?
- Profitable in all areas of the business? Just some areas if so, which? At the expense of everything?
- By when? Tomorrow? Next week? Next year? In 10 years time?

Fig.2.6 Developing specific objectives

People often try to avoid using all the SMART criteria when setting objectives and the one most commonly avoided is the time-bound one. There are usually two reasons for this. The major one is that setting yourself a specific date to complete an objective opens up the possibility of failure. As we try to avoid failing it is easier to just keep extending the deadline. The second reason is simply 'sloppy thinking', which is why people often say 'as soon as possible'. If you set the time as 'as soon as possible' then you can always get out of it by saying to yourself 'It hasn't been possible yet!'

Setting a deadline for your objectives is essential if you want to be effective in your planning and implementation.

Specific

Often one of the hardest things to do is to make an objective specific enough. People think they know what they want and feel that because they have a clear idea of what is to be achieved, everyone else will know as well. Figure 2.6 provides an example of how to make an objective more specific.

In Figure 2.6 the overall objective is to be more profitable, which is fairly meaningless until we know the answers to the questions posed. To take the objective to extremes, more profitable could be by £1. Until we do know the specifics everything we do will be vague and lacking in direction. An objective of increasing profits by 50% within 6 months will require very different priorities and actions compared with an objective of increasing profits by 10% within 2 years. In other words, the specifics within the objective drive the priority and the behaviour of everyone working to achieve it.

If you have a vague objective you can often clarify it by asking yourself 'What does that mean?'

Measurable

Objectives must be measurable so that we know how well we are doing. Most things that we do are measurable so checking that our objectives are measurable is important. It helps you make them more specific and easier to plan for.

For example, improving communication as an objective is difficult to measure, but holding monthly staff meetings is easy to measure. Increasing profit is easy to measure, but to say increasing profit by 5% is much more effective because you have a figure to aim for. You are either ahead, on target, or behind. If you are behind, you either do something different or you change the target.

Figure 2.7 shows how you can look for ways of measuring objectives.

Achieveable and Realistic

Some people have difficulty clarifying the difference between achieveable and realistic (the R in SMART).

The simplest way of explaining the difference is to consider whether an objective is achieveable by assessing the skills, knowledge and abilities of the people involved (the internal factors). As a contrast, the objective may or may not be realistic because of the external situation, the environment and the factors influencing the situation.

For example, an objective of converting the practice to fully private may well be achieveable because of the clinical and management abilities of the staff. However, it may not be realistic because of the local economic climate, a patient base of 98% exempt patients and the fact that 23 other practices in the town are attempting the same thing.

Time-bound

We need deadlines to perform. It's that simple. Most people work to deadlines. Deadlines must be realistic, and specific. For very short deadlines the time is required. 'Please have the recalls done by Friday' may mean different things to two people. To the person doing the recalls it could mean that the recalls

Some examples of how to make objectives 'measurable'
1. Patient satisfaction – use patient questionnaires.
2. Staff motivation – use appraisals or staff turnover rates.
3. Marketing to increase patient numbers – use telephone call enquiries (or all enquiries) or number of new patients.
4. Periodontal disease improvement – use periodontal indices.
5. Development of staff – use qualifications and appraisals.
6. Efficiency of practice – use questionnaires and/or number of patient complaints.
7. Time-keeping on appointments – how often do you run late?
8. Appropriate recruitment and selection – use responses to adverts, length of stay for staff.

Fig.2.7 Measuring objectives

must be completed any time up to midnight on Friday. To the person issuing the deadline it could mean recalls need to be done for the 4pm post on Friday. 'Please have the recalls done by 4pm Friday' is fine.

People want to avoid deadlines because this makes the objective 'real' and also sets up a possible failure situation. As long as you can avoid a deadline you can never fail. Unfortunately this also usually means the objective will not be achieved because other activities will intervene and you can always put your objective off a bit longer.

Most deadlines should have a specific date not in a 'months' time, so you know exactly where you are. If you state 'to set up a system for effective practice meetings in a month's time' then you can always look at your objective and mentally fool yourself into saying 'I've still got another month'. Believe us, people do this all the time. To be effective the date must be exact.

So, our original (and vague) objective to improve communication becomes:

> 'We will set up regular monthly structured practice meetings where everyone on the staff is involved in discussion and decision by September 30.'

Note that this objective is very specific, even down to the fact that everyone on the staff will be involved in both discussion and decision. It is obviously measurable in that either they are monthly or they are not. It is achieveable (we hope!) and we believe it is realistic and it is very clearly time-bound.

Now all we have to do is work out how we are going to achieve our SMART objectives — and that is where tactics are involved.

Success indicators

These are indicators on how well you are doing. They may be financial indicators, behavioural indicators (how often is something being done? are people meeting standards of behaviour?), response indicators (how often do you get certain types of response?) or some other form of measurement.

Tactics

Tactics are the day-to-day tasks you need to do — making a telephone call, writing a letter, designing a brochure, etc.— that will result in the objective being achieved.

Dentists often make several false assumptions when it comes to tactics:

- They assume they must be able to undertake the task themselves, even if they ask someone else to do it
- They are poor at paying for (investing in) expertise outside the practice
- They neglect to delegate as often as they should.

One of the problems with strategic thinking is that the objective seems so broad that you never get around to doing anything positive towards achieving it because the task is so large. Few people would ever attempt to get started because it appears so overwhelming they wouldn't know where to start.

Conclusion

A mission statement will help tell you what the business is about — or more precisely, what business you are in. If you are unsure as to why you are in business then it may be easier to work this out by considering your strategy and objectives first. Working through these clarifies thinking.

Sometimes you must work on immediate objectives or a general strategy because circumstances require something to be done now. The danger is to continue working like this rather than making time to think out the main reason for being in business.

Important Note
There are times when tactics, fire-fighting, must come first because we have no choice. However, if you are always fire-fighting you lose control of your own direction.

Also, you often have to adopt a tactical approach at first while you work on your strategy. Part of this involves collecting and collating management information about the practice because strategic decisions about the future should not be made without appropriate and adequate information.

What am I selling?

3

Marketing is a balance between what you want to sell and what people will buy. We will start by considering the 'selling' side of this balance because it is important, in marketing terms, to be totally clear about what you are hoping to sell to patients. If you cannot describe it easily, then you will have difficulty selling it. As a reminder of how this fits into our Marketing Cycle, Figure 3.1 illustrates where we are. We are still on the first question.

It may seem as if we spend a lot of time looking at this first stage compared with the other stages. This is because the answer to the initial question of what you are selling depends on knowing what you are trying to achieve and what your potential customers want to buy. In order to find out the answers you need to gather fairly detailed information and do some focused thinking. That is why the initial stage is so critical and important.

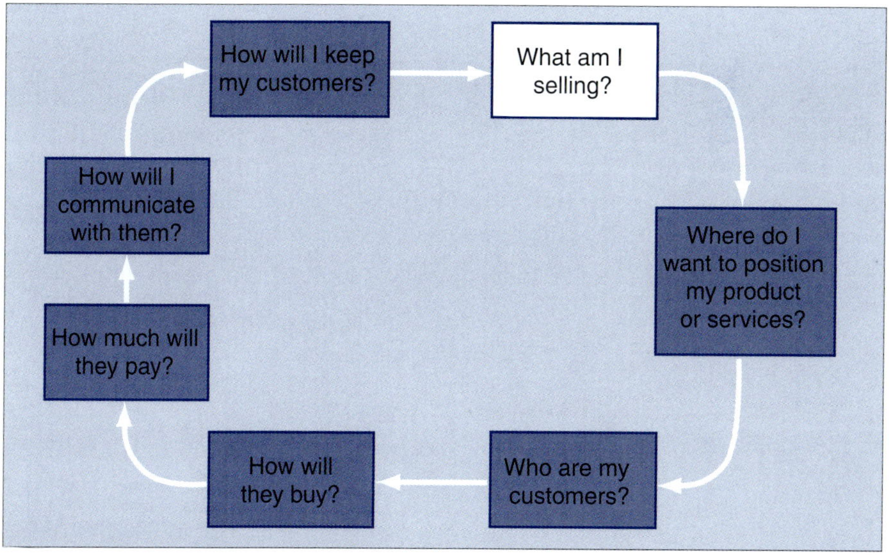

Fig.3.1 The marketing cycle

Different perceptions of dentistry

In the past most practices (and the people in them) have tended to assume that what they are selling is so obvious that they have taken it for granted. Yet if we were to ask a number of different practices what they thought they were 'offering' patients we might find their answers to be illuminating — and almost certainly different from each other.

For example, many dental practices would probably say they were selling 'dentistry' or 'dental care'. Some might say they were selling 'dental treatment', while others would define their products as 'fillings, dentures, crowns and bridges'. Still others would say they were selling 'preventive dentistry'. Specialist practices would regard themselves as selling 'endodontics', 'orthodontics' or 'crown and bridge'. Some would define their product as 'family dentistry' while others would say 'NHS dentistry' or 'private dentistry'.

All these answers might mean something to the practices, but would probably be seen by their patients as something very different. After all, what is 'family dentistry'? What do patients think 'preventive dentistry' is? Is the patients' perception of the meaning of family dentistry the same as the practice's? Do patients appreciate the difference between 'oral health' and 'dental care'? For that matter, do dentists understand the difference — and is the difference the same between different dentists?

We also have to consider that what dentists mean by these terms may be different to the staff's understanding, and may even differ between different dentists in the same practice. Finally, while dentists tend to regard their products and services in clinical terms, patients often buy the non-clinical aspects of the total dental experience more than the dentistry itself.

All of this leads to the inescapable conclusion that we tend to have a hazy understanding of exactly what we are selling. Yet we must have a very clear grasp of what we are selling if we are going to market the practice successfully.

In marketing terms, we have to be able to:

- Define precisely the product(s) or service(s) that we intend to sell or are selling
- Describe their unique selling propositions (USPs), features, benefits and advantages over our competitors.

Defining your product or service

It is clearly important to define a product or service precisely, not only to enable prospective funders (like the bank) and patients to understand what you intend to do, but also to ensure that you set clear and achievable objectives. Clear objectives are paramount to good business clarity and success. The more focused you are about what you are selling and who you hope will buy it, the easier and more successful your marketing strategy is likely to be.

In dentistry, it is tempting to think that offering everything to everyone — which is what general practice means to many people — would be the most popular option. In the early days of the NHS when there was a shortage of dentists and most people needed substantial dental treatment this was probably true. Now things are different. Patients have become more demanding and their expectations are higher. Many people need less treatment because there is less disease. The generalist is no longer needed in the same way as in the past, and dentists need to start thinking about how best to refocus their practices to meet the changes in patient needs and expectations and still meet their own personal clinical ambitions.

Good marketing allows you to meet both of these sets of desires or wants, not just fulfilling patient expectations, or providing the dentistry you want to do regardless of changes in patient requirements. Good marketing has an eye to the future, so that your practice can anticipate future changes at an early stage. In other words, you need to try to forecast what people will want in dental and consumerist terms over the next few years.

We can consider how we work out the answers to these questions by looking at two models commonly used in marketing:

- The PESTE analysis
- The four Cs

The PESTE analysis

As shown in Figure 3.2 PESTE stands for political, economic, sociological, technological and environmental. Your analysis tries to estimate what changes in the enviroment are likely in these five areas.

Political changes

The political changes occurring now and in the future will obviously affect a

Political
Economic
Sociological
Technological
Enviromental

Fig.3.2 The PESTE analysis

practice and what it trys to offer patients. It applies to both the main political changes (will the current government win the next election?) and local politics (what is going to happen in your area after the next council elections?). It also applies to the changes happening in dental politics, for example, the move towards the expanded use of professionals complementary to dentistry and the growth of 'high street' dental clinics. You will need to look at all of these and decide how they will impact your practice.

How will government changes and policy affect the area? Are there opportunities to offer a different type of dentistry or to focus on a speciality? Should attracting a local specialist to the practice be considered — or perhaps terminating an agreement with one currently employed? What will happen if a 'high street' dental shop opens adjacent to the practice?

All these questions affect your marketing strategy, and all revolve around a refocus of the dental services you think are the right ones to offer in the future.

Economic changes

Naturally, political changes will affect economic factors. Will another term for the current government mean a dramatic change in inflationary pressures? Will local decisions affect the prosperity of the community? You have to use the information available and best guess to try to estimate these kinds of forecasts.

However, you also need to look at the general and local economic situation to make some of your estimates. Will changes in the nearest town, such as parking, access or development, mean an increase or a decrease in the disposable income of your patients? Are there likely to be major redundancies in the area, and is that good (extra cash) or bad (no other jobs)? Will the possible attraction of 'cheaper dentistry' in other practices entice your patients away?

These considerations and any others of an economic nature will form part of your PESTE analysis.

Sociological changes

There are a number of major sociological trends that are happening now and will apparently continue. There will be more older people around in the future. The birth rate is currently declining. More women go to work outside the home. People wait longer before starting a family and there is a great interest in being more 'healthy'.

Do you know what is happening to your area, and socially to your patients? Do the trends seem to be the same in your locality, or are there local differences? Are you likely to see the development of areas designed for young families, a commuter society that tends to look for their dentistry elsewhere, or a return to traditional family houses?

All these factors also affect the patient base, and need to be considered. We will look at this in more detail in chapter 4.

Technological changes

We live in a time of rapid technological development, not just within dentistry but also outside it. How will digital TV and the Internet affect your patients and their buying habits? Is it necessary to advertise on the world wide web, or will your reputation continue to attract patients? Will new advances in dental imaging become an important feature for patients in the future? Will patients expect to receive their recalls via e-mail? Will major refurbishment be needed to bring the practice up to date?

Environmental changes

The importance of the environment in business planning and implementation has increased recently. Dentistry is no exception. The role of mercury in amalgam, the constant discussion over water fluoridation and the disposal of waste are just some of the issues that may influence your decisions for your product or service.

Besides these more obvious concerns we need to be aware of what is happening in our vicinity, in the country and internationally. What enviromental trends may affect our buisness as we start this new millennium?

The PESTE analysis is part of the process of marketing, which enables you to:

- consider the questions above and other relevant issues
- try to think of the 'right' answers for your practice and your locality
- match these answers to your objectives for your practice
- analyse the type of 'dental service' you think it is appropriate to provide.

The four Cs

The PESTE model is one way of trying to anticipate the requirements of customers in the future. A second model that helps us think about what we plan to take into account in our marketing strategy is the 4Cs model shown in Figure 3.3.

Customer

Knowing who your customers are and what they are likely to want is a vital part of market research. It also affects how you will position your practice. Both of these topics are covered in more depth in chapter 4.

Consumer Reaction

We can consider consumer reaction from two main perspectives — local consumers and consumers in general. A knowledge of what is going through people's minds and how they are thinking will influence what may happen as a result of what you either do or fail to do.

For example, suppose you decided to change an aspect your practice, such as its location or the hours it opens. You need to know how people will react to the change. This doesn't just mean how patients will react, but how consumers in general will react. Moving the location of the practice may result in a drop in patient numbers but an increase in new patients who can now access your practice more easily. If the new patients are the ones you wish to

Customer

Consumer reaction

Cost

Competition

Fig.3.3 The four Cs

attract then this could be a good decision. If the new patients are not then moving the practice might be unwise.

Similarly, changing practice hours might seem like good sense to you but not to the customers. One practice that was planning to attract more private patients thought that extending evening hours was a sensible decision. The practice was close to the train station and the dentists assumed that business commuters would welcome the opportunity to attend for their dental appointments on their way home. However, some fairly basic market research was carried out first and the findings suggested that nearly all the people asked preferred to continue visiting a dentist near their work during the day because in the evening all they wanted to do was get home. An expensive mistake was prevented by checking on consumer reaction first.

The other area to consider is how consumer reaction is changing generally. We all know that we, as consumers, are expecting more from those who provide services, especially more in the way of customer care. We tend to lose patience with companies who keep us waiting on the telephone, we expect more from shop assistants and we no longer blindly accept instructions from professionals without some kind of explanation.

Cost

In your marketing strategy you need to consider how your fees (or prices) match the perception of cost in the minds of your existing and potential customers.

Marketing involves calculating the fees you need to charge to ensure you make an appropriate profit with the costs people expect to pay. In some cases you may not feel you can offer certain services because the expectations of the potential market are too low and you are not confident you can attract sufficent sales. Most importantly, you must have an accurate idea of how much it costs you to provide your services. Alternatively, your marketing objectives and strategy may change. We will look at this when we consider the marketing mix in chapter 5.

The competition

Marketing people often worry about the competition. Is this relevant to dental practice, or are we members of a profession who do not need to compete with each other?

The answer is — it depends. While many dentists do share a helpful, supportive and professional relationship with their colleagues, an element of competition often exists in reality. The new NHS practice that opens in town can be a real threat to a mainly private practice nearby. The new branch of a chain of practices under the umbrella of a corporate body is usually considered to be a competitor to the old-established family practice.

But the answer is more complex. Who exactly is your competition? Do you have competitors in your own business (in other words other dentists) or is your main competition the other businesses that are after your customers' money? Are your patients attracted more by the holiday brochures, the advertisements for new cars and the attractive restaurants in town than by your practice brochure or your advertisement in the local paper?

In reality, both are important. If you have a dental practice in the high street and another one opens up offering cheaper, better or more attractive services (such as more accessible opening times, comfortable waiting area, new equipment) then you may find some patients moving across to the new practice. They will be the ones attracted by such things, and not necessarily by better quality dentistry.

The other competition (shops, holidays, cars, restaurants, etc) also want to attract your patients and in many cases they do — unless you can make sure your patients understand and appreciate that you are offering a service they really want.

How can dental practices compete successfully? The answer is by ensuring that you define (and promote) what is special about you, your unique selling proposition (USP), and focus heavily on the benefits of what you are selling rather than the features.

All the factors involved in the PESTE and 4Cs models will affect your decision as to what you are selling. You cannot hope to begin marketing successfully before clarifying the answer to this question.

What makes your practice different?

Having given some thought to what patients are likely to want now and in the near future, and the sort of service your practice can provide, you need to start turning your thoughts into tangible benefits that can be communicated to existing patients and the potential patients you want to attract.
Consider these questions:

- Are you providing general dentistry, or is your practice specialised?
- Will you have a preventive approach or a restorative approach?
- What does a preventive approach mean?
- Are you catering for patients of all ages, or will you emphasise family care, care for children, care for the elderly, the provision of emergency care and so on?

The more specific the answers to these questions can be, the easier it will be to manage your practice and confine development within your own objectives. The more specialised you are (or the clearer you are about the type of dentistry you wish to provide), the easier it will be to attract the right patients for your practice.

These questions need to be a mix of what you would ideally like to do (in dental terms) with what the community in the surrounding environment is likely to want and pay for. This applies to all forms of treatment, regardless of the funding mechanism you choose. For example, a high quality practice specialising in implants might find it more difficult to market itself when sited in a remote country village or in a city council estate. While it can be done — and certain individuals do succeed in building successful practices in the most unlikely places — it is easier to match the practice with the environment. Similarly, a family practice might find it more difficult to develop in the middle of a complex of city roads where parking is difficult compared with a family practice just off the high street where parking is easy and the practice is near the bus route.

All of the above is only half of the equation. The other half is about your patients. Who are they and what are they looking for? We will cover this in chapter 5.

Your Unique Selling Propositon

In sales terms a USP is the unique selling proposition. In other words — what is different about you that is likely to be important to your patients?

Modesty often prevents practices from identifying their USP. Every dental practice has a USP in its approach, because every practice is a reflection of its partners or principal, and is different from any other. However, is this unique enough to be a selling proposition and is the approach sufficiently clearly defined? One dentist believed his patients all came specifically to see him — until he moved his practice to a new site away from the bus route and lost a third of his patients.

Identifying your USP can be a difficult and painful process, which can involve market research among the patients as well as a great deal of questioning, self-analysis and discussion among the whole team. Until you have identified the USP and put it into simple words that everyone can understand, you will have a problem promoting it. If you cannot identify one then perhaps you should take this as an opportunity to create a USP that appeals to patients. Of course, this assumes you know the requirements of your patients in the first place. How to achieve this is the subject of chapter 4.

A useful way of looking at the definition of your USP is to consider what the practice is offering from the patients' point of view, rather than the professional's viewpoint. The more you get into the patients' shoes the easier you will find it to adopt a true marketing approach.

What do people want?

4

One of the major challenges for any business is recognising that what customers want is not necessarily the same as what they need or what the business person wants to provide. This is especially true in healthcare, where providers of care feel they have a mission to satisfy the needs of the population and can sometimes assume that people will obediently fall into line with their suggestions. As we all know, we do not always do things that are in our best interests if they conflict with our desire to do something else.

A vital part of marketing is finding out what people really do want. Not just in terms of what they will actually buy but also in terms of how they will access the service, how they will purchase the product, what hidden costs are involved, what other priorities exist and conflict and what is happening in their peer groups and so on.

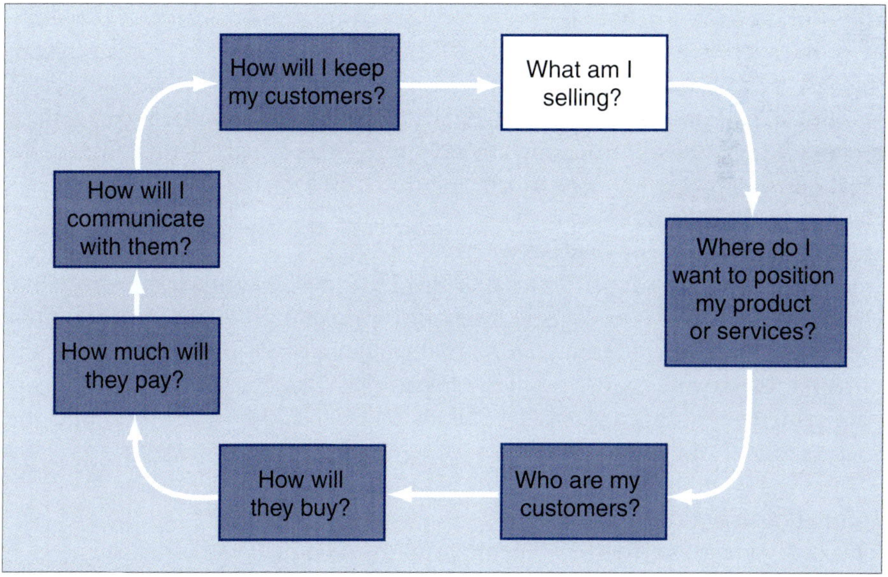

Fig.4.1 The marketing cycle: what am I selling?

All of this can be classified under the blanket heading of 'market research'.

With regard to our progress round the Marketing Cycle we are still at the first stage. This is data we need to collect before we can answer our initial question: what we are selling? (Figure 4.1).

Basic areas of research

Many people think that market research only means looking at patient requirements usually in some form of questionnaire. This is obviously very important, but market research should encompass a lot more. Figure 4.2 lists the main areas that should be considered.

You need to be aware of what is happening within the practice itself as well as outside. In the last chapter we considered the PESTE analysis in broad terms, but now we are looking at what is actually happening around us, especially locally. How will local planning developments affect our business? What is happening in the local schools? What percentage of our patients pay privately and is that increasing or decreasing? All of these factors need to be taken into account before we can start to plan.

Besides looking at these areas in more detail we will also consider where you need to go to discover the answers. Sometimes the information is readily available such as within existing records but sometimes you may need to seek the help of an outside agency to provide you with data. As with all aspects of running a business you need to decide when it is more cost-effective to engage a consultant or similar agency and when to discover the information for yourself.

Information about the business

Information about your practice or organisation is usually readily available, especially if you have management accounts or a computerised system within the practice. The sort of information that we can glean will include: where our patients come from, how much they spend within the practice, what our most profitable treatments are, the frequency of attendance of patients and the success rate of our recalls.

Information about the locality

This is a wide area (Figure 4.3) and you may well decide to engage external assistance to provide this type of information. You can find much of it from

The broad areas of market research for a dental practice
• Information about the business
• Information about the locality
• Information about the direct competition
• Information about indirect competition
• Information about the patient base
• Information about patient requirements

Fig.4.2 Sources of information about the locality

Basic information on the locality
• Locality of the practice
• Demographics of the area
• Population changes
• Employment changes in the area
• Socio-economic trends
• Work patterns in the area
• Future planning for the area
• Home ownership trends
• Commuting and travelling patterns
• Transport plans for the area
• Communication trends

Fig.4.3 Types of data on the locality

council offices, the local library, local estate agents, the chamber of commerce and the Citizen's Advice Bureau. Other helpful activities include informal conversations with people in the locality, for example transport staff, shoppers and local schools. People living and working in the area possess a rich diversity of knowledge and information which can be tapped into by asking the right questions.

It is sensible to divide all this data into sections such as the headings in Figure 4.3. These headings are useful, and will start to give you ideas about what the people in your locality do, what they want, when they want it and how they currently try to get it. Are people mainly working full-time or part-time? Is there a significant proportion of people on shift work? Is local industry healthy or at risk? Are more people owning or renting their homes? Are people leaving the area or attracted to it? What are the age ranges of those moving into and out of the area? What is the birth rate trend? Are there plans for a new bypass or motorway? Will public transport improve or deteriorate?

Information about the direct competition

Direct competition means other dental practices in the area. We looked at this

Information about the direct competition

- What are the fees and can I see them?
- How easy is it to contact reception?
- What emergency service do they provide?
- How long before I can be seen?
- How easy is it to make an appointment that suits me?
- Are they easy to get to by public transport?
- Can you park nearby easily?
- What is the local reputation of the dentist(s)?
- Do they answer the telephone at lunch time?
- How do people sound on the telephone?

Fig.4.4 Direct competition

Information about the patient base

- Number of patients in the practice
- Patterns of attendance
- Distribution of patients
- Age ranges of patients and trends
- Payment trends

Fig.4.5 The patient base

in chapter 3. Figure 4.4 lists some of the areas you might want to investigate in the direct competition, but is by no means exhaustive. Note how the areas covered are all from the viewpoint of the patient and will differ from the kind of things you (as a dentist) might be looking for. You may wish to organise your thoughts by carrying out a SWOT analysis on each of the practices in your area.

Information about indirect competition

In some ways this information is harder to collect because indirect competition is basically everything else on which people choose to spend their money. Holidays, entertainment, cars, clothes and gadgets are all items that people want to buy.

If you study spending patterns then it is no secret that people also spend money on health and beauty, both areas that involve dentistry. Perhaps a possible answer is to reposition your practice so that it is perceived as part of the health movement rather than part of medical provision. We shall examine the role of positioning later and in chapter 6. Some practices are already doing this by focusing on appearance and health rather than on repairing dental disease. The successful ones are doing it in response to the identification of an appropriate local market for such services.

Information about the patient base

Figure 4.5 looks at some basic information about your patients that will help you in your analysis. You need to know where your patients tend to come from (by postcode ideally) as this will help provide indications of their buying preferences. You can find further information on what people in certain postcodes are likely to spend their money on from organisations that specialise in this, but this can be very expensive.

Perhaps of more value is the knowledge about whether there is a movement of certain age ranges within the practice. Is the average age of patients getting younger or older? Are you attracting more couples with young families, or more single people who commute to work? Are payments for treatment rising in both amount and speed? Are more people attending regularly, or do you attract more emergency patients who attend once and are never seen again? Are any of the dentists or hygienists suffering from increasing failed appointments?

All of these questions need answering if you are to work on your marketing plans, and almost all this information is available to you within your practice itself.

We shall be looking at this more closely in the next chapter.

Information about patient requirements

Mention the term market research to most dentists and they immediately think of a patient survey about the reception or waiting room. We hope to put this rather limited approach to rest but we do not want to give the impression that patient surveys are not valuable, important and fairly easy to do. We believe they are a vital part of your marketing strategy, not only because they will provide important information but also because they tell your patients you are interested in their views.

You may decide to engage an external consultant to do a survey for you, or you can use a pre-packaged survey. You may decide to design your own. We would encourage you to prepare or have prepared a bespoke survey, as it will focus on the real issues on which you need to gain patients' views.

However, the advantage of using other surveys is that they have already been prepared and tested for you, so it saves you time. The disadvantage is that they will be generic instead of specific to your practice and, if provided free, will

Hints for patient surveys

- Keep it short (one side of A4)
- Make it easy to understand
- Make the questions clear
- Do not ask something you are not prepared to change
- Use closed questions
- Use a Likert scale (1-5)
- Pilot them to check your mistakes
- Evaluate after making any changes

Fig.4.6 Guidelines for patient surveys

contain questions that are relevant to the person providing the survey and the data about your patients will be the price you pay for the survey. If you decide to commission someone to do it for you then you must know clearly what you want to ask first so you can instruct the consultant appropriately. This method is the most expensive in terms of cost, but a good marketing consultant with dental knowledge can be an excellent investment if instructed well.

The essence of patient surveys is to pick a single subject and make your questions short and easy to answer, preferably on one side of A4 paper using yes/no answers or ringing one number on a scale (called a Likert scale) to provide an answer. You will need to pilot the questionnaire on about 10 patients first to make sure they understand the questions. Figure 4.6 contains some guidelines for a patient survey, and really underlines how easily you can run one for yourself on about 50–60 patients: a good representative sample for the average dental practice. It is important to ensure that the questionnaires are given out fairly, ideally to the next 50 patients that come to reception or attend for an appointment. Questionnaires should be coded for different dentists if there is more than one at the practice, and whoever is handing them out should not just give them to the

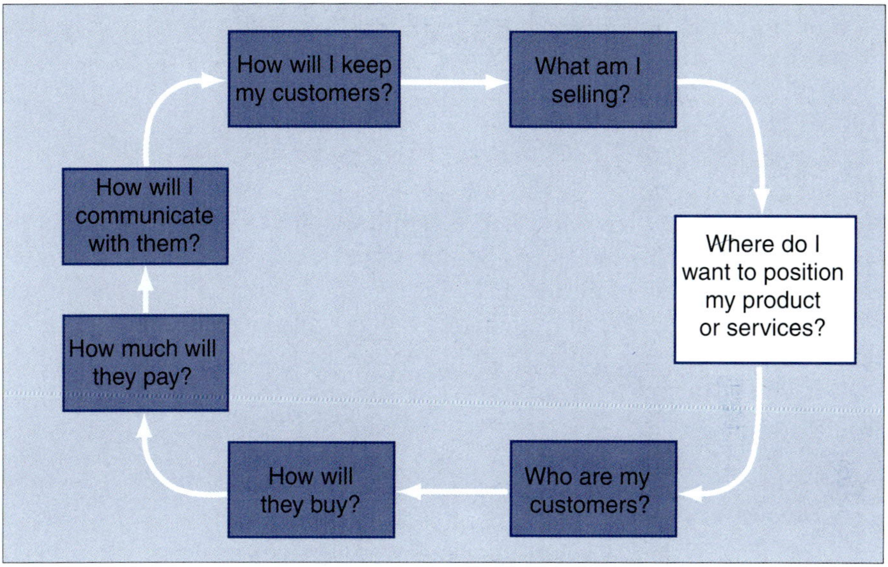

Fig.4.7 Positioning products and services

people he or she thinks would be best suited to answer them.

Patient surveys cannot always provide extensive information when carried out like this, but a number of short surveys carried out at intervals will provide you with a lot of very useful data. If you want to survey in depth then using a consultant may well be the best route to follow.

Whichever type of survey you use, make sure you follow it up by asking patients again after you have made any changes to the practice in order to evaluate how effective the changes have been. You should also ensure that you do not ask questions about areas you have no intention of changing, as this is not only a waste of time but is insulting to your patients.

Positioning your product

Having collected all the information appropriate and relevant we can consider the next stage in the Marketing Cycle — how we wish to position our products and services (see Figure 4.7), in the light of what is realistic given the nature of our local market. One way of doing this is to analyse all this data within a convenient marketing model known as the '6Ps', which covers price, place, promotion, product, people and position. We will be looking at this in depth in chapter 6.

Conclusion

If objectives are balanced with patient requirements then it is important to identify the requirements of patients as accurately as possible. This can be achieved by a number of means, including identifying general trends in an area which could help identify the requirements of potential patients. This becomes increasingly important when planning changes to business objectives which may involve attracting a different set of patients to those that currently attend the practice.

Who are my customers?

5

This chapter looks at the people who are most important to survival in business — customers. From a marketing viewpoint, we are asking the simple question: who are they and who would you like them to be?

In the marketing cycle we have moved on to look at the important questions of who our customers are and how they will buy our products (Figure 5.1). Note we have moved past the question about positioning your products or services. The question of market 'position' is a complex interplay of customers, quality of product or service, external marketing forces, competition, demand and price. All of these factors interlock to allow you to determine, define and consolidate your position. We will be looking at this in more detail in the next chapter.

It is only if we examine these questions in detail that we can start to formulate a sensible plan to effectively communicate what we do.

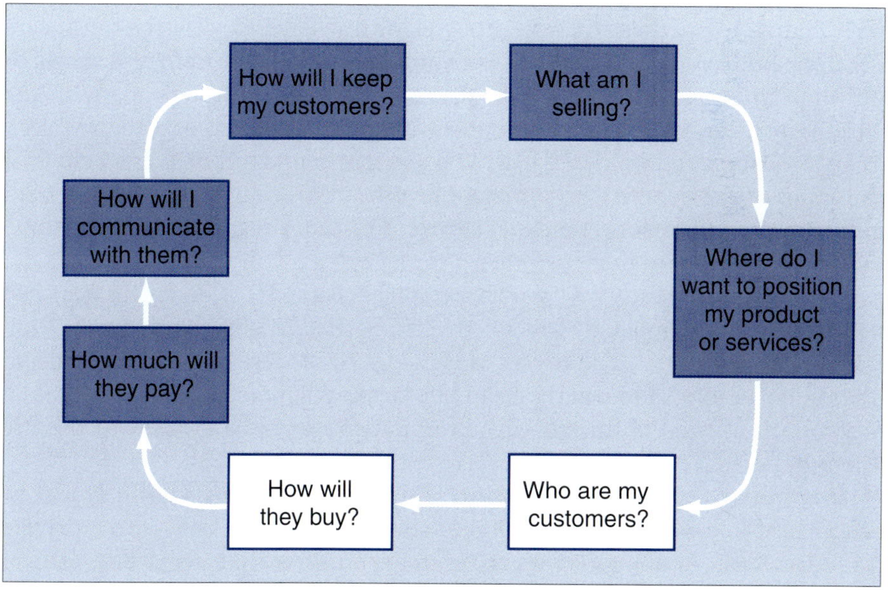

Fig.5.1 The marketing cycle: who are our costomers and how will they buy?

Only by understanding as much as we can about our target market and our customers can we formulate and frame those messages and package and present our service in a way that is attractive to them. Marketing is essentially about communicating certain messages in certain ways in order to make an appropriately designed service sufficiently attractive to them that they wish to buy it. If we do not know enough about our customers we make dangerous assumptions about what causes them to buy our services rather than those of other professionals, or other things altogether, products that they might find more attractive than dentistry. Knowing our customers means that our communication with them, and our marketing plan, will be much more effective.

Patient, client or customer?

Before we start to examine the patient base we need to clarify terminology. In healthcare, customers are usually referred to as patients rather than customers or clients. In marketing terms customers are the people who buy your products or services. Some professions prefer the term 'client' because it carries a sense of status with it, and they consider the term 'customer' too bald.

In marketing terms it may help to consider the patient as a customer however they choose to purchase their healthcare. Most patients pay for the healthcare services they receive through NI contributions, through insurance schemes or through direct payment to the healthcare provider. Although many in the healthcare arena are still uncomfortable with the concept of the customer rather than the patient, in an increasingly consumerist marketplace, it can help us if we think of the people who purchase healthcare from us as customers, with particular requirements and expectations. This can assist us in framing some of our approaches to that customer.

Thinking over the last few years has changed. Patients are no longer expected to be 'patient' and hopefully few practices think that patients should be 'grateful' to get NHS treatment. The advent of choice in healthcare, and therefore seeing the patient as a consumer and a customer means that practices and other dental organisations need to think more about patients as individuals with specific buying choices.

If some of this seems irrelevant, consider this — marketing is just as important to an NHS practice or a hospital department as it is to a private practice. One of the key aspects of marketing is that good and ethical marketing assists in managing patient expectations so that people buying their healthcare do not have unrealistic expectations of standards of care, both clinical and non-clinical.

Analyse your patient base

Although we briefly looked at this in chapter 4 we need to be aware that one of the first steps in marketing is to know your current patient base as well as possible. These people are, after all, the people you have so far attracted to the practice. Only when you have fully analysed your current patient base can you really identify the sorts of patients that you would like to attract more of and formulate an action plan to do so.

Who are they?

What are the profiles of your patients in terms of age and background? Although we may feel uncomfortable in trying to categorise patients in this way, most organisations have a clear idea of the socio-economic backgrounds of their customers. Try to build up a picture of your average patient, and work out the percentages of patients in each age range and background.

Doing this will give us a clear picture of where the majority of your patients 'sit' in terms of their profiling, and what your current marketing effort might be doing to attract them. Your current marketing will be attracting that type of patient. This is all well and good if these are the patients you want more of. It is less good news if these are the patients you would prefer not to be treating in your practice — for whatever reason.

Additionally, knowing their lifestyle is important. Are they commuters, people at home, retired people, people with children, people without children, people with high-pressure jobs, people for whom time is money? The more of these questions that you can answer, the more focused your ultimate marketing plan will be, and thus more successful.

Many people try to embark on a marketing plan without the necessary information, and wonder why it is not particularly successful. Doing so is similar to planning and carrying out a course of dental treatment without a proper medical history and consultation.

What is the most profitable part of your patient base?

What are your most profitable lines of treatment, and which portion of the patient base buys them? This is essential information when we come to targeting some of our marketing messages to our patients. If you have a computerised practice management system, this data should be relatively easy to extract. We are not going to use this data to the disadvantage of our patients, but simply to focus some of our communications to reach the sorts of patients we would like to attract, and promote aspects of our treatment in a positive and ethical way.

Where do they live?
This is an important question, and the answer can save hundreds of pounds and many hours spent in fruitless and expensive promotion in the wrong areas to the wrong people. The type of housing and post code can also give strong and useful clues to other aspects such as socio-economic background and people's values.

What are their values?
This may seem an unusual question, but these days more and more large companies are designing advertising and promotion campaigns, as well as complete marketing strategies, to appeal to specific sections of the population with certain sets of values. If you can find out what drives your patients, what is important to them — what their values are — then you can frame many of the messages you wish to about dentistry in a far more effective way.

At a base level, this is examining why your patients buy dentistry. Is it for reasons of security. Is appearance important to them? Do they feel that being at the leading edge of treatment is important, or do they prefer an old-fashioned, personal approach? Do they hold strong feelings that NHS treatment should be available for all, free at the point of delivery? Do they hold views on the availability of private healthcare in general? What is their current level of knowledge about dentistry?

What sort of lifestyle do they have and where do they go?
This is essential information if you are considering promoting the practice in your area. Where do prospective patients go in their spare time (or even in their working time)? What sort of publications do they read? What marketing communications do they currently take note of? Where do they go that you could consider using as a vehicle to promote your practice?

How do they spend their money?
This is linked with the lifestyle question. Apart from 'distress purchases' (exciting things like petrol and cat food) what do patients prefer to spend their money on? If you know the answer to this, you have some idea as to what you

are competing against, whether it is holidays or vet bills. This is all useful information when looking at what we want to communicate as well as how we are going to communicate.

What are their expectations?

This is a tricky question. When one works in the dental environment all of the time, it is difficult to remember how little many of our patients know about the benefits and value of dentistry. It is highly unrealistic to expect even regular attendees to know that dentistry and clinical techniques have changed. Generally, dental practices seem to overestimate their patients' knowledge of dentistry and how practices work.

Consumer reaction

All of the information outlined above will prove very useful but it is essential that we also determine what our current patients — and particularly those we wish to react to and find more of — think of our service. Finding out about your patients goes far beyond simply asking about their likes and dislikes in the practice and if they would like to have the waiting room redecorated. You need to gather data that will show you your ratings against a number of elements of your service, both clinical and non-clinical. For example, you may wish to run a survey of your patients which includes questions about how you rate on explaining costs of treatment as well as asking what people think about the fee levels for private care. A carefully planned patient survey will help in giving you vital information about what your key patients like and dislike about your level of service — information that you can use to redefine and alter your service to make it more attractive.

Remember that the aim of the exercise is to gather information, particularly from those patients we have identified as the sorts of patients we wish to retain, and who we would like to more of. This leads to the difficult question 'Which patients am I prepared to lose?' If promoting services to a particular section of the community, this will inevitably mean that the messages are inappropriate for another section of that community, some of whom will be your patients.

How will my patients buy?

The final question is how your patients will pay for the services you want to provide. This is not just a question of how much they will pay — but how they will choose to pay.

As with everything else so far, the answers will differ according to the patients you have and their experiences and expectations. In an exclusive private practice some patients will still expect to be sent an account after treatment is finished. Other practices will find patients paying in cash. Money is an emotive subject, and the methods used to pay for services and products are still steeped in tradition and expectation.

This information should be added to everything else you have collected in order to decide how effective different methods of payment might be in changing cash flow and increasing profitability. While the image of your practice is still very important you may find you can reduce your need to provide invoices for a lot of patients by offering other incentives without sacrificing the professional 'feel'.

Conclusion

Choosing the types of customers you want and then identifying ways of attracting them to your practice is an important benefit of a successful marketing approach. The old-fashioned way of simply setting up your plate and coping with all comers is no longer necessary. Marketing enables us to segment the market more by aiming for certain types of patients with certain dental needs and requirements.

Getting the plan right

6

So far we have examined a number of issues that we need to clarify before undertaking marketing activity. These have included understanding what it is that you are trying to sell, understanding the nature of your patient base and being clear about what it is that you are trying to achieve (your SMART objectives). We now turn our attention to the marketing plan. The document that sets out what we are intending to do to market the practice and how we will go about it.

Many practices do not have any sort of plan; carrying out promotional activity without a clear idea of what they are trying to achieve, sometimes incurring considerable expenditure. How many practice brochures are written without a clear objective in mind and without a true picture of the target patient? How many are unclear in what they are trying to say and communicate? Without clarity of vision and understanding, much of the effort put into producing something like a brochure is likely to be wasted. Getting your planning right means that you will be directing your efforts at the right people, in the right way, at the right time and probably being more cost-effective.

If we return to the Marketing Cycle we have reached the stage of deciding how to position ourselves in the market (Figure 6.1).

The marketing plan

The marketing plan is a key document in the success of a practice. It is important that it is written down, so that things do get done and, to act as a brake on enthusiastic but unfocused ideas for promotional activity which, although attractive in the short term, will not contribute to achieving the objectives that you have. How often does a promotional idea present itself which, although initially attractive, proves to be waste of time in the long term? For example, an excellent rate offered by a sales person from a business telephone directory might seem to be a good idea and a great bargain. However, if your plan is to attract a higher proportion of patients wanting periodontal

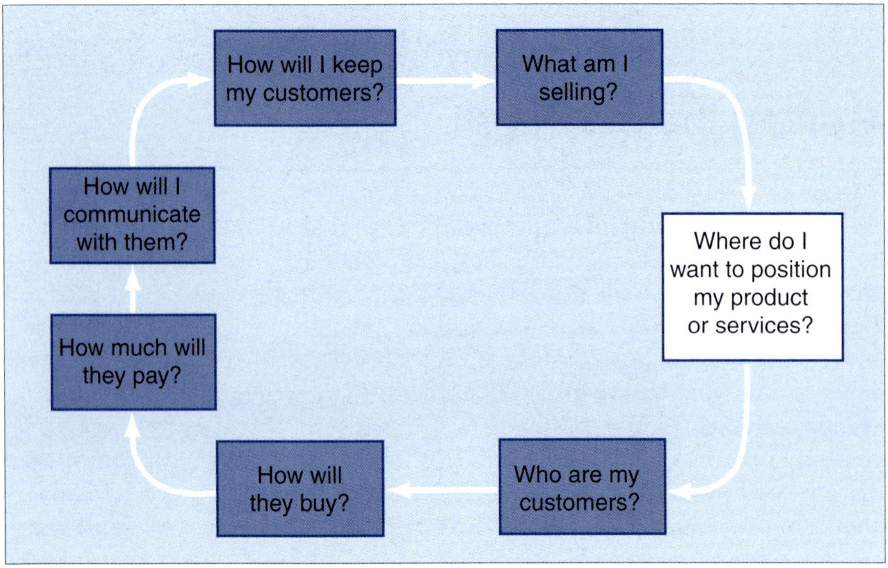

Fig.6.1 The marketing cycle: positioning yourself in the market

care, an advertisement in a publication to which people go when they have an emergency may not be the most appropriate way to spend your money.

Having a written plan means you have a reference point against which you can judge the validity of the new ideas that arise from time to time. Some may be valuable, some not, but you will make a better quality decision with the overall plan as a benchmark.

What should go in a marketing plan?

The marketing plan does not need to be particularly lengthy, but it does need to address the questions in Figure 6.2. You can use these as a checklist to test how effective your own marketing effort is at the moment. We will consider these in further detail later in the chapter

The importance of research

We have considered some of these issues already. Clearly, it is essential that we have done our homework in terms of finding out about our customers, who they are, what they buy, why and determining what our own product or service is within

The marketing plan
• What are our marketing objectives? • What message are we trying to communicate? • What is our USP (unique selling proposition) as a practice? • Who are we trying to communicate with? • What are the most appropriate ways of communicating with them? • How much resource are we prepared to put into this in terms of time, and money? • How will we know if our marketing effort has worked?

Fig.6.2 What should go in the marketing plan?

the practice in clear terms before we can embark on a planning exercise. This element of research is not just an one–off exercise. It is important to remember that the environment in which we operate is constantly changing. Areas change, demographics change, even the way dentistry is offered and delivered is currently changing to a much greater degree than many people foresaw. Our research must therefore be an ongoing process if we are to keep one step ahead.

The marketing mix

Many writers say that the marketing plan should consider the six 'Ps' of what is known as the 'marketing mix'. These are:

- Product
- Price
- Promotion
- Place
- Position
- People.

Product

The plan should state what sort of dentistry you are offering and give an idea of the overall level of service and care you provide. It is dangerous to assume that anyone new coming into the practice and asked to implement the plan will necessarily know without it being made explicit.

Is there a consistent message across clinical and non-clinical areas? For example, you may have a high-tech surgery with the latest equipment, but if you have no means of allowing patients to pay by swiping a credit card then

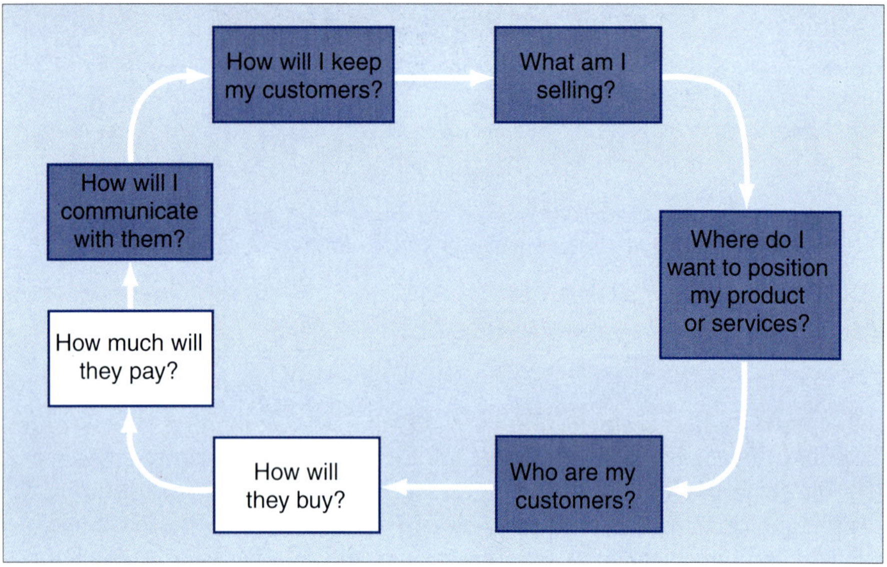

Fig.6.3 The marketing cycle: how much will they pay?

your product will not be clearly defined.

Price

The plan should cover the pricing structure. This may seem a strange item to include as part of the marketing mix but it is an essential judgment criterion for patients or customers. Prices or fees will give people an idea of the level of service offered and give out a message about the sort of care provided. Most people consider setting fees as a purely financial decision. However, in our view it is a strategic marketing decision.

Price is an important aspect in the marketing cycle because it is sensitive to local and external factors as well as internal decisions. As can be seen from Figure 6.3, how people buy and how much they will pay are important questions. Are your fees perceived as expensive or cheap in your area? Patient perceptions will differ in different areas of the country according to a whole variety of factors. What value is being offered for the fees set, not just in clinical dentistry but also in the area of non-clinical care? Most importantly, is it appropriate to the level of fees being charged? It is as dangerous, in business

Factors influencing fees

- Location
- Volume
- Costs
- Competition
- Image
- 'Added-value' services
- Accessibility
- Speed of delivery

Fig.6.4 Factors influencing the level of fees charged by a dental practice

terms, to provide too great a standard of service for too low a fee as it is to provide too low a standard of service for too high a fee.

In the UK these questions apply as much to predominantly NHS practices, where prices are already set, as they do to fully private practices. Marketing is about managing and fulfilling patient expectations. Defining your service levels, and pricing these appropriately, is one of the key areas of marketing that many practices neglect. Your perceived prices will be a major factor in allowing patients to determine the level of value you offer and whether or not they wish to buy. They also say a great deal about your image. Some of the factors influencing your fees are listed in Figure 6.4.

Promotion

This is what most people think of as marketing. But as we have seen, it is only one part of a much wider process. We shall be exploring methods of promotion in the next chapter. What is important is that they earn their keep. Promotional methods need to be selected and implemented based on their ability to deliver the results you have decided you want, rather than as a blanket 'let's promote the

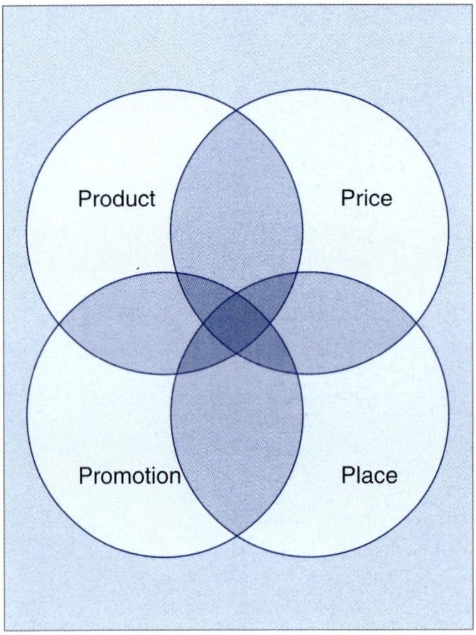

Fig.6.5 The marketing mix.

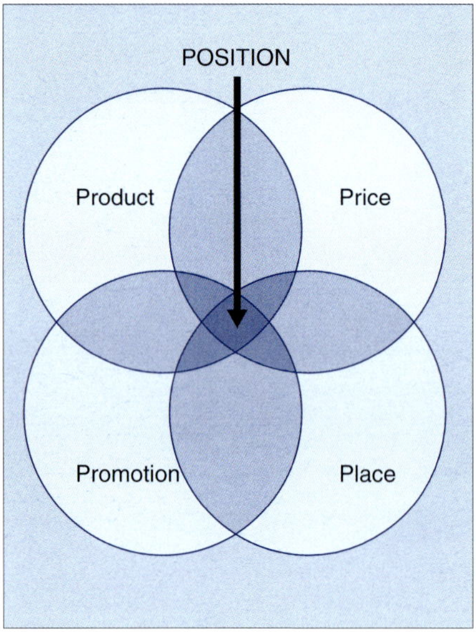

Fig.6.6 Position; the fifth P.

practice'. Without due care and attention, promotion can backfire badly, giving out the wrong message to the wrong people.

Place

This means not simply where your practice is located but also how and when services are offered to patients. Is the practice accessible? Is it easy to make appointments? Are appointment-making facilities available at times when patients might want them? Over the lunch period, for example, does a practice rely heavily on an answering machine with no message-leaving facility, and then expect patients to phone back at a time more convenient to the staff?

Position

We can represent these basic 4 Ps as overlapping circles (Figure 6.5) but the fifth P (position) can be represented by the areas of overlap in the centre (Figure 6.6). Positioning your business is an important part of the overall plan, because it gives more focus to all the other aspects and, as the diagram suggests, is made up of all the other Ps.

For example, a practice that positions itself to provide rapid, innovative oral

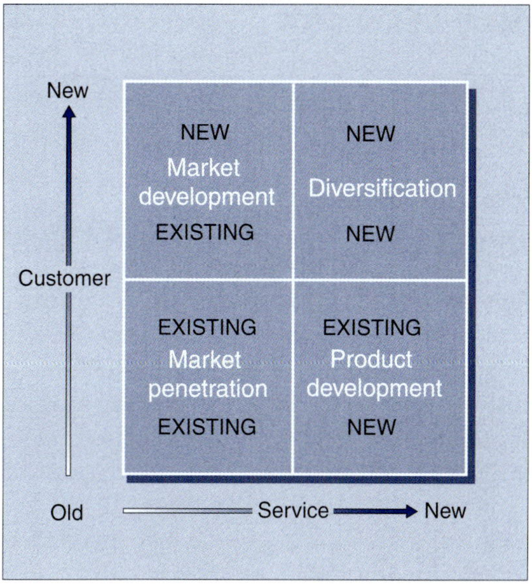

Fig.6.7 The Ansoff Matrix

care as part of a dynamic health programme for busy business people in a city centre will need to look at its products, prices, place (parking, venue, opening hours, etc.) and promotion in a very different way to the traditional family practice providing reliable dental treatment on the outskirts of town.

People

The sixth P involved in the marketing mix refers to the people who are involved in marketing the practice.

Who is going to make this plan happen? It is pointless preparing a plan without working out who is going to be responsible for which part, delegating appropriate tasks or giving people the resources (time and money) to make sure that it happens. Are your staff appropriately trained? Do you have sufficient expertise in-house or would it be better, less time-consuming and more cost-effective to employ the services of an expert in copywriting, for example? Marketing plans will not implement themselves. A clear action list is needed and appropriate people identified to implement the various parts.

The key elements of the plan

At the beginning of the chapter, we set out the key questions that a marketing plan should address. These are set out in more detail below.

What are our marketing objectives?

Before we can consider our objectives, we need to consider, in broad terms, our strategy. The four options available to us are depicted in Figure 6.7, the Ansoff Matrix. In simple terms we have four choices. We can sell existing services to our new customers, or new services to existing customers. Our other choices are to sell new services to our existing customers and finally new services to new customers. Obviously we can also try and do any combination of the four choices.

The relevance of the Ansoff Matrix to our marketing plan is that it provides us with a clear idea of what we are doing and how we need to promote it to our customers. We would need to do different things to market our product to different potential customers. This is why a single brochure may not succeed if a dental practice is using it to retain existing patients and attract new ones. The messages you need to put into the brochure should differ according to which box in the matrix you are relating it to.

Having made this decision we need to set marketing objectives. Just like business objectives, these should be SMART: Specific, Measurable, Achievable, Realistic, Time-bound.

An objective may be to increase the numbers of patients attending the practice: for example, 'to increase the patient base by 30% by 30 September 20--'. This is a marketing objective because it is about attracting new patients to the practice. Similarly, we may decide to 'attract 10 new patient enquiries a week during the period 1 June to 30 September 20--'. Both of these are explicit, tell people what the marketing activity is intended to achieve and are eminently measurable — essential if our marketing effort is to be effective.

Other marketing objectives may include increasing the proportion of a certain type of dentistry bought, achieving more appointments for the hygienist and so on. Simply saying 'To promote the hygienist's services' is pointless. Why do you wish to promote his or her services?

Another area where people say they want to use marketing is in order to 'raise the profile of the practice'. Although this is valuable, how will you measure it? To whom do you wish to raise the profile? What do you want to achieve by doing so? Convincing answers to these sorts of questions are needed for a sensible marketing plan that will contribute to the success of the practice.

One of the most basic questions is 'are we aiming to attract new patients or retain existing ones?' In reality, the answer is probably both. In marketing terms this means that you will need to consider different activities and different messages for two sets of people.

What message are we trying to communicate?

It is sometimes difficult to crystallise what we want to say. You will probably be communicating different messages for different groups. You will also want your message to reflect the image of the practice. Very often, practices try to use one method of communication to cover lots of different messages to different people.

A prime example of this is the practice brochure combined with a patient information leaflet (PIL). A PIL has a particular purpose, often very different from that of a brochure. The PIL is required to give certain information about practical aspects or features of the practice. It is, quite literally, for information. While a brochure does this to a certain extent, it should be focused far more on the patient and the benefits that they may perceive in coming to the practice. We shall be examining features and benefits, and the difference between them, in greater depth in the next chapter. The message however is clear. Make sure that you are saying the right thing, to the right people, through the right medium.

What is our unique selling proposition as a practice?

We make no apologies for returning to this again, having mentioned it in chapter 3. This is very important for all who work in the practice. No two practices are entirely alike, and you need to determine what makes you different, what makes you special to your patients and how this is communicated. Do not assume that what you come up with will be entirely new. There are many practices offering 'high-quality dentistry in a relaxed and friendly environment.' It may be that you provide dental treatment in a sophisticated and elegant environment. Whatever it is that makes your practice's personality, be prepared to articulate this and use it in your marketing material.

Dentistry is in an increasingly competitive environment. Practices that have thought through why they are different and why patients should come to them as opposed to any other practice will find it easier to meet that competition.

With whom are we trying to communicate?
You should be able to answer this question having considered the issues raised so far. If you have a clear idea of who you are trying to promote the practice to, then your messages in the many forms of promotion available to you will become easier to identify and formulate.

What are themost appropriate ways of communicating with them?
We will be considering this aspect in more detail in the next chapter. However, it is clear that promoting the practice via the local schools may not be the most effective way of attracting patients over the age of 65. Giving this question proper consideration will mean that you may spend less time and money on promotion, but it is more likely to be effective.

How much resource are we prepared to put into this in terms of time, people and money?
The plan will inevitably require time and probably some money. It is sensible to set a budget for the planned activities. Doing this will also allow for reflection on whether any particular activity has been value for money. An expensive advertisement that brings in only two maintenance patients may not be a wise investment. Alternatively, the same advertisement that brings in two patients for extensive treatment may be. This brings us to the final question.

How will we know if our marketing effort has worked?
If we want to be effective in our marketing, there is little point in undertaking anything unless we have a means of knowing if it has been effective or not. Evaluating the efficacy of our marketing is essential for the next stage of the planning process, and allows us to determine more appropriate ways of achieving our objectives in the future. Of course, the key is having clear measurable objectives. What sort of patients do we want to attract? What sort of dentistry do we want to carry out in our practice? What rate of flow of new patients into the practice do we want? These are all sensible questions, the answers to which will drive our marketing strategy.

Promoting the message

7

We have almost moved full circle in the marketing cycle, and Figure 7.1 shows that we have reached the stage of identifying the most appropriate ways of communicating our marketing messages to our patients, whether new or existing. This is achieved by using promotion, one of the 6 P's mentioned in the last chapter.

A definition of promotion

In this book we have considered what message you are trying to communicate, to whom and for what purpose. Often, people think promotion is marketing,

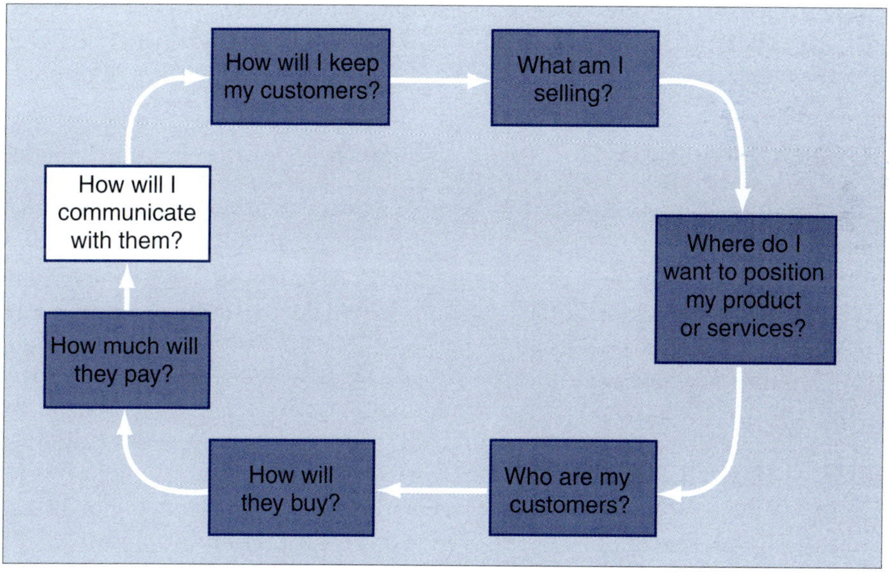

Fig.7.1 The marketing cycle: promotion

although as we have seen from the previous chapters promotion is really a link in a chain, which will help us to achieve our specific objectives.

Promotion involves getting your message to your market. Different methods of promotion will be applicable and appropriate for different purposes and for different people at different times. It is no use expecting a brochure to communicate what we want to say to both existing and new patients, across a wide age and socio-economic range.

Promotional methods need to be selected and implemented based on their ability to deliver the results required, rather than simply to promote the practice as a means of attracting more patients. Dentists too often take a generalised approach to promotion. For example, they react to the need to increase patient numbers without considering to whom they wish to promote the practice, what messages they wish to promote and how cost-effective it will be. This is where planning, an understanding of the Marketing Cycle and the answers to the questions we have been posing in the previous chapters, become so important.They emphasise the importance of all the other stages before we communicate with our market.

Promotion inevitably involves thought, time and very often money. This makes it even more important to be sure the right and most effective methods are chosen. An opportunity to advertise at a special rate in the local paper may appear attractive at first glance, but may be inappropriate if the kind of patients you wish to attract tend to discard the local paper in favour of some other form of reading.

Notes for the wise

Not all methods of promotion work in all practices. If a local practice has found one method of promotion effective it does not mean it will be effective for another practice's patients and objectives. Another important aspect is that most promotional methods have a life cycle. What may be effective for a few months may not be so effective in the long term. Evaluating the success of your promotional activity is not just desirable — it is essential if you are to gain maximum value for money. For example, before renewing an advertisement in the local telephone directory we should know how many new patient enquiries were generated over the previous year. How many of those enquiries were converted to new patient appointments? If this information is not being collected, then it would be a good time to start. Promotion should work and be cost effective.

The usual methods of promotion favoured by dental practices
• Advertising • Direct mail • Press releases • Advertorial (articles that look like editorial in magazines, but are in fact paid for like advertisements). • Exhibitions • Open days • Personal visits • The Internet

Fig.7.2 Methods of promotion

Methods of promotion

Figure 7.2 shows a summary of the methods dental practices can use to promote the practice or to communicate their message.

Advertising

Many small businesses, including dental practices, claim that they have spent very little on advertising for years. Often one of the reasons is that they feel they are not making enough profit and that they cannot afford to advertise or promote their practices. Alternatively some dental practices feel no need to advertise. However, with the increasing change, competition and choice in dentistry, promotion for the practice that wishes to be successful, retain patients and attract new ones is essential.

In dentistry, advertising is still considered undesireable at best and unethical by many. This is partly due to the ban on professional advertising which was in place in the UK until the 1980s, and partly due to the old-fashioned notion that the only professional way to get new patients is by personal referral. While personal referral is still one of the most effective ways of obtaining new

7: PROMOTING THE PRACTICE

LEGAL, DECENT, HONEST, TRUTHFUL

7.1 A dentist may only use publicity or advertising material which is legal, decent, honest and truthful and has regard for professional propriety. Responsibility for all publicity and advertising in relation to a practice rests with the dentist.

NAME OF THE DENTIST TO BE INCLUDED

7.2 All advertisements and printed material relating to a given practice should include the name of at least one dentist normally in attendance at the practice in question. Advertisements in a foreign language should include the name of the dentist in the form in which it is listed in the Dentists Register. However, the name may also be written in the language concerned.

UNACCEPTABLE CONTENT

7.3 Publicity or advertising material should not:

(i) be of a character that could reasonably be regarded as likely to bring the profession into disrepute;

(ii) make a claim which is not capable of substantiation;

(iii) contain any reference to efficiency, skills or knowledge of any other dentist or practice;

(iv) make a claim which suggests superiority over any other dentist or practice;

(v) recommend a specific product

Fig.7.3 Acceptable forms of promotion

patients, it is not the only way. Figure 7.3 is an extract from the General Dental Council's *Maintaining Standards*, which clarifies for the UK what is, and what is not, acceptable for all forms of promotion.

Costs

Advertising and promotion need not be expensive. One has, however, to accept that some of the expenditure will not have results. Large firms, thinking in terms of advertising appropriations and campaign budgets, use a variety of national media to get their message across to the public. The majority of dental practices will think in terms of modest sums, carefully spent to the best advantage, and so may be best served by local media.

Fig.7.4 The AIDA sequence

Advertising effectively

Effective advertising involves three essential factors.

- The right copy.
- The most appropriate form of media.
- The right timing and frequency.

For advertisements to work you must have good 'copy'. Put simply, this means that the wording and layout of the advertisement are critical. A good advertisement follows the AIDA sequence (Figure 7.4):

- Attracts Attention
- Arouses Interest
- Creates Desire
- Stimulates Action.

Unless you are an expert don't write your own copy. You may know more about the product or service than anyone else does but leave it to the experts to convert the information into a good advertisement.

Most dentists tend to write about what they think their patients are interested in. This is usually not what patients want to read at all. Some brochures written by dentists promote the technical aspects of dentistry rather than the benefits to patients.

Features versus benefits

Many people are confused by the difference between features and benefits. A good advertisement should focus on what the patient will get from the service (the benefits) rather than what the service is (the features). Dental practice owners are often proud — and rightly so — of their investment in equipment, their level of service, qualifications, and such like. However, these are all features of what they have to offer. What interests all of us as human beings (and by definition our patients!) is what the product or service will do for us. These are the benefits, and should be promoted in your advertising copy.

You must choose the right media for the people you want to attract. To attract new patients, different media will be used to those used to bring new services to the attention of your existing patients. What type of newspapers and magazines do the target patients read? Are the target people the most likely to read the free local weekly paper? Or is the practice interested in patients who read the glossy, monthly county magazine? If an advertising agent is not going to be employed to advise on the choice of media, some more research will need to be done. What are the publication's circulation figures? Where is it sent if it is a delivered paper, where is it sold if purchased? What are the circulation trends? Is it successful or failing? Is it the sort of publication you want your dental practice to be seen in? Does it reflect the positioning of the practice?

Traditionally dental practices restrict themselves to the Yellow Pages and occasionally the local paper. Some with ideas on the target market will place advertisements in appropriate magazines. Whatever the medium chosen — which could include county magazines, school publications, local church, religious or community publications and estate agents' maps given out to house-seekers new to the area — make sure the practice is seen in the place most looked at by the target market.

Finally, advertisements must appear at the right time and with the right frequency. One advertisement is rarely effective; repetition is essential for successful advertising. Keep the practice name in front of potential customers. It is not easy to measure the effectiveness of advertising. One way of doing so is to include a code number in the advertisement to be quoted by patients when

Basic rules for writing a good press release
☑ It should contain the information; what, who, where, when and why within the first paragraph.
☑ It should have a catchy title which suits the publication.
☑ It should be no longer than one side of A4.
☑ It must also contain a contact name, address and telephone number. This should be at the bottom of the sheet after the word ëendí.
☑ It is worthwhile including a relevant black and white photograph, with a caption typed on a piece of paper and stuck to the back of the photograph. Photographs help to ësellí stories.
☑ Give the press release a date.
☑ Do not underline anything in the body text.
☑ Give an embargo date if necessary. (A date before which the release cannot be published).
☑ Include a quote where possible.

Fig.7.5 Writing a press release

calling the practice. Another is to train all of your staff to find out and record how new patients found out about the practice.

Features of a good advertisement

Print advertising can be divided into three separate parts:

- the design or illustration
- the headline
- the body of the advertisement.

Design or illustration is the part of an advertisement that catches the attention. The headline should be attractive, not necessarily short (10 words is not too long) and should help to pinpoint the target audience. The body text should sell the service and invite a response (telephone number, address, opening hours, and so on). The body should be written in clear, short sentences.

Embargo date

No longer than one side of A4

BDA
WORKING FOR DENTISTRY

Embargo: 00.01 hours, Tuesday 8 September 1998

DENTISTS CALL FOR £150 MILLION FOR NHS DENTISTRY

Appropriate catchy title

In evidence to the Review Body on Doctors' and Dentists' Pay, the British Dental Association is calling for £150 million a year for NHS dentistry over the next three years. This would meet the Government's objectives of improving access and modernising the service. Extra funding is needed to increase the number of dentists working in the NHS and to provide up-to-date equipment.

What, who, where, when and why in first paragraph

The BDA is also calling for an increase in dentists' fees by at least the Average Earnings Index. This is needed to help maintain dentists' earnings in line with similar professional occupations. Dentists working full time in the NHS have suffered real terms decreases in their incomes as their earnings have not kept pace with average earnings over the past five years. If their earnings had kept pace, income before tax would be £5000 more. The consequence of this is that there is a shortage of NHS dentists.

Despite Government assurances that the NHS will continue to be available to all those who need it, many people do not have access to an NHS dentist. Budget cuts in the Community Dental Service have lead to job insecurity, posts being frozen or unfilled. As a consequence, the dental care of the most vulnerable people in the community is threatened.

Dr Bill Allen, Chair of the BDA's Council, said:

"Dentists do not leave the NHS for ideological reasons. They leave because they cannot cover their practice overheads nor spend an adequate amount of time with each patient. This has resulted in a shortage of NHS dentists in many areas of the country. Sufficient incentives must be provided to retain dentists who are currently working full time in the NHS, as well as attracting back those who have reduced their NHS workload."

Relevant quote

ENDS

Shows end of press release

For press enquiries contact Kate Cinamon at the British Dental Association's Press and Parliamentary Department on 0171 935 0875 ext. 243. Out of hours, Kate can be contacted on 0171 693 6958.

British Dental Association
Press and Parliamentary Department
64 Wimpole Street, London W1M 8AL
Telephone: 0171 935 0875 ext 243/258/299 • Fax: 0171 487 3024
E-mail: press.parliamentary@bda-dentistry.org.uk • URL: www.bda.dentistry.org.uk
Registered Office as above. Limited by guarantee (14161) England

Contact name, address and telephone number

Fig.7.6 An example of a well-written press release

Layout is particularly important. People normally read from top to bottom, so putting the most attractive part at the top makes sense. Hence, illustration, headline, body, in that order from the top will attract the customer's attention.

You also need to promote the unique selling proposition of your practice — something special and distinctive about your practice which sets it apart from others. Remember patients will be interested in the benefits of attending your practice so state them clearly in your advertising.

Writing a press release

One of the least expensive forms of sales promotion is the public relations approach. A well-devised press release may attract far more attention than an advertisement at far less cost. Articles can be written for the local paper, even letters to the editor can be a way of making a practice's name known to potential customers.

The problem with this form of sales promotion is that unlike buying advertising space, there is no control over whether or when the story will be printed. As with advertising and direct mail, it can be worth paying for the services of experts. A good public relations consultant, if you can afford one, knows the right media and can put your story across in an attractive way for the editors.

Press coverage is often a free method of communicating with potential customers through a medium which might otherwise have been too expensive. Essentially it is a simplified news item concerning your practice written from a 'news' point of view. The press release must be newsworthy and interesting enough for the editor or journalist receiving it to use. Remember that the journalist is your first target audience for the release. Journalists receive many releases every day, so there is no guarantee of publication.

If you are thinking of using this form of promotion then you must ensure you have a story to tell which is newsworthy. Sponsoring a local football club or school sports team is a possible opportunity but that in itself is hardly exciting news. Inviting a local celebrity who might be a patient to open your new surgery or children's area, or launch your sponsorship of the school rugby team, is news and could result in some free publicity in the local paper. Similarly, winning a dental award or a national award (such as Investors in People) is another ideal opportunity for a press release and also offers a photo opportunity. Figure 7.5 summarises the main points in writing a press release and Figure 7.6 is an example of a press release.

The Internet

There is no doubt the Internet is a growing medium for promotional activity, especially now we can access it through digital television. Many dental practices are already taking advantage of some form of web page and patients are beginning to look for dentists via the Internet. However, the full potential of the Internet, and how it can be used to communicate with patients, has still to be fully exploited. Having a web page can mean a great deal more than simply transferring all of the text from a brochure to a screen. The possibility of contacting your patients by e-mail could be considered. Soon patients will be able to make their own appointments electronically via the web, accessed through the television in their living-room.

A web page can be designed by people at the practice, usually using space provided by an Internet service provider (referred to as an ISP) as part of the practice's subscription. However, like other forms of promotion, expert help will usually produce better results. Currently, costs for web page design vary so be sure to get quotes from several designers.

The Internet is still in its infancy. It is adviseable to maintain at least a watching brief, even if this form of promotion is not considered necessary at the moment. Many patients will expect a dental practice to embrace Internet technology as it has been by the rest of the business community. Keeping in touch via the BDA website or the recent BDJ book *The Internet Guide for Dentistry* will help you assess its potential and suitabilty for your practice.

Events

One method of promotion is the practice open day. This can be linked to a national event or a practice can run its own event and advertise it locally. Before embarking on this course we need to consider what it is trying to achieve for the practice. Is it trying to increase general awareness and raise the profile of the practice? Is it to attract new patients? Is it to bring back lapsed patients? Knowing the answers to these questions will help to develop a much more focused and profitable event.

Guidelines to help ensure that patients will recommend you to their friends

- Ensure patients know you are accepting new patients and that this message is communicated by all the staff. The most common reason for patients not to refer others to their dentist is because they think he is too busy.
- Ask your patients for more referrals (and ideally get all the staff to ask as well, following suitable training).
- Provide excellent clinical dentristry.
- Provide excellent non-clinical care in all aspects of the patient visit.
- Learn good communication techniques so you can explain to people what is going on, involve them in decisions on treatment and make them feel they can ask for help and will be listened to.
- Focus on the patient's needs and wants, not on your advice.
- Keep your staff well-motivated. Motivated staff mean a happy atmosphere, and people notice this when they visit.

Fig.7.7 Seeking recommendations

Brochures and other literature

Never overlook the importance of internal promotion. What do the practice's letterheads, business cards, logos, brochures, name badges, etc., say about it? The design and quality of these items say a great deal to patients and reflect on the practice image in a powerful way.

One of the most common forms of written literature is the practice brochure. This is not the same as the patient information leaflet (PIL). A PIL is intended to give information about NHS services as required by current statutory regulation. It is not a marketing device. A brochure can and should be, by focusing on the benefits of the practice's services for its target patients, a powerful form of promotion. Many brochures fail because it is not clear what they are intended to achieve. Are they intended to attract new patients? Are they intended to reassure existing patients? Are they intended to sell specific treatments? Knowing the answers to these questions should direct their content, how it is written and how and where the brochure will be distributed. Clearly this cannot be achieved unless we first have clear marketing objectives.

Practice image

Practice image is often fairly low on the agenda in promotional campaigns but it is one of the most powerful methods of promotion available. People keep appointment cards, show letters to friends, talk about their dental visit and recommend you to their friends and relatives. If you want more personal recommendations then you need to work on a practice image that communicates to everyone what type of practice you are.

Given the choice between two adjacent shops selling the same goods, do you buy from the dimly lit shop with peeling paint and dirty windows, or from the clean, brightly lit shop with an attractive frontage? Most people prefer the latter, even though the other shop may have lower prices. A clean, bright shop attracts more customers. Clinical skills may be of the highest order, but patients will consider that to be reflected in the physical state of the practice. Many patients remember the waiting room and reception area (on which many practices spend the least amount of care and attention), and notice very little in the sparkling surgery itself. The higher costs of maintaining the better image in the reception areas can be a real investment rather than simply an expense.

The image of a business is a picture in the mind of the customer and it is created mainly by senses of sight and hearing. With the arrival of the high street dental practice chain (corporate bodies, some of whom are already high street names, are becoming involved in dentistry) the practice image will become more and more important, especially the exterior of the practice. Retailers have known this for years. The public will come to expect certain standards of exterior, reception and surgery. Ignore this change at your peril. Patients will be attracted by the bright exteriors and uniformed staff. Ultimately, the standard of dental care will be most important in patient choice but the role of image will inevitably increase.

Personal recommendation

Personal recommendation is one of the most effective forms of promotion. However, like all the others mentioned, it is wise to make it happen rather than simply hoping it will happen.

Asking for referral can be quite difficult for people to do, especially at first. Scripts are usually fairly useless, however, having an idea of what to say is helpful until people gain confidence and the words come naturally. Figure 7.7 provides some guidelines for helping you improve your ability to seek recommendation.

Setting a budget

It is difficult to be prescriptive about how much should be spent on promotion but a typical figure that many businesses use is 3% of turnover. On a turnover of £100,000, a promotion budget of £3,000 would be reasonable. This percentage may seem high to most dental practitioners, but remember that it is an investment in the practice and, if carried out effectively, will stimulate additional income.

Besides, a budget that has been worked into the figures in advance means that everyone feels that the money is there to be spent, rather than feeling you are taking money from other areas of expenditure. Psychologically we prefer to spend money because we have decided we want to spend it, rather than because circumstances are forcing us to spend it. Budgeting is an important part of marketing, and should be under the control of the owners of the practice, not financial advisers.

Conclusion

Promotion is the way we communicate with our market, and providing you have considered all the aspects of the Marketing Cycle first you should find that your promotional methods are communicating the right messages. How to choose which method of promotion is partly common sense and partly experimentation to find out what works for you.

Keeping your customers

8

The final stage in the Marketing Cycle is the answer to the question: how can I keep my customers? (Figure 8.1) The answer lies in the concept of customer care.

Customer care is the delivery of an appropriate service for patients based on all the information we have gleaned so far in our marketing activities. It is important to remember that marketing enables us to balance the requirements of our patients with the operating environment in which we work. Thus the emphasis on customer care should be appropriate to our objectives, our circumstances and the expectations of our patients.

What is a customer?

Customers are people who have 'requirements' for a product or service. Given

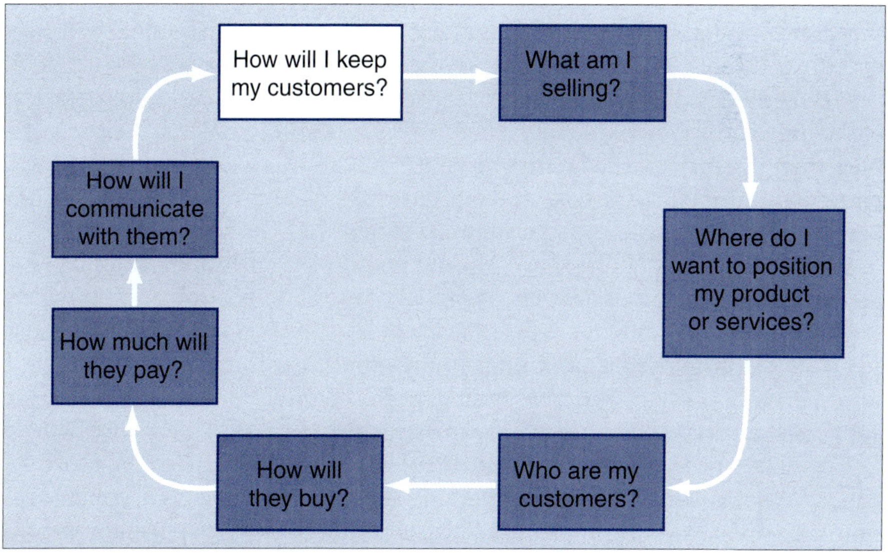

Fig.8.1 The marketing cycle: how can I keep my customers?

Reasons for buying
• Convenience • Choice • Access • Availability • Perceived value • Status • Impulse

Fig.8.2 Factors affecting the decision to buy

What is a customer?
• A customer is the most important person in this practice. • A customer is not dependent on us we are dependent on him or her. • A customer is not an interruption to our work but the purpose of it. • A customer is not someone to argue or match wits with. Nobody ever won an argument with a customer. • A customer is a person who brings us his or her wants. It is our job to handle them profitably.

Fig.8.3 Defining a customer

the choice, and assuming they are paying for the service, customers will part with their money to the supplier who offers them the best value.

We are all customers of suppliers and we make our choices on purchasing based on a number of factors (Figure 8.2). Market research helps us to understand which of the factors in Figure 8.2 are the most important for a particular group of customers, and our customer care processes should ensure that we deliver or exceed what customers expect.

Figure 8.3 looks at how we should view our customers and behave accordingly. We must all have encountered organisations or businesses which seem to make life as difficult as possible for the customer, businesses that almost seem to have employed a 'sales-prevention' officer. Customers expect a quality product, but it is a happy combination of a good product with friendly, efficient support staff that determines an organisation's success.

Customers need developing over time. The more we are given, the more we expect. What you give today as something special will be analysed, copied and improved upon by your competitors, it will become the expected norm tomorrow.

Far too many practices make assumptions that they know what the patient wants. Patient's, or customer's needs, wants and expectations change over time. It is very easy to get out of touch.

Dental practices are only just beginning to understand the concept of 'customer care' and put some basic principles into operation. For many professionals, customer care is still quite a difficult concept due to an attitude that assumes patients will accept what they are given and be grateful. That will change as people's expectations change.

Patients or customers ?

In recent years there has been a tendency for organisations think of those using their services as customers in order to try and focus more on the concept of customer care. The same is happening in dentistry. People are referred to as customers rather than patients to help shift the emphasis away from the more paternal approach towards the more 'sharing and service' approach. The belief is that if we refer to patients as customers more often, we will find it easier to focus on the non-clinical aspects of dental care. Experience shows that when we think of a 'patient' we are more likely to be thinking clinically, despite all the attempts to think of patients as whole people and not just mouths.

However, if you feel more comfortable with the traditional term, feel free to replace the word 'customer' with 'patient'. The principles of customer care apply — whatever you call the person buying from you.

Effective customer care

To the customer, the measure of a good organisation to do business with can be broken down into three areas:

- the quality of its product
- the ease with which you can do business with them
- how pleasurable an experience it was dealing with them.

In other words quality in:

- Product
- Process
- People.

Quality of the product

When we use the term 'product' we are not referring to a set of dentures or a crown, despite the fact that these are obviously products. We are really referring to the dental visit in its entirety, from the moment the patient first contacts the practice to make an initial appointment until the final closing events — payment of the bill or setting up some form of recall.

We can consider the quality of the product to include: the patient's perception of how easy it is to contact the dental practice at a time that suits them, how easy it is to make an appointment time that is convenient for them, how easy it is to reach the practice and (if appropriate) park nearby, what it is like entering the building and so on. Figure 8.4 includes a full list of components for the dental visit.

'Excellent', 'good' and 'the best' are all emotional words that are comparisons with known experiences. To ensure that a product is good, comparisons should be made with similar products and services recognised as being superior by the marketplace. This does not only mean comparisons with other dental practices but other health-related products and services as well. What is it like visiting the doctor? How efficient is the local optician? Why do people use the high street optical store? Visits to other organisations and subscriptions to trade magazines will help investigate the competition. A product or service must be compared with the market leader.

It is very easy to sit in your practice and believe that you have an excellent product and because it is so good customers will want to buy it. In reality you can only be sure that you are providing what the customer wants by speaking to them and doing quality market research.

Contacting a dental practice at lunchtime, for example, can be quite difficult if it closes and only has an answerphone providing an emergency number and opening hours. People who can only ring at lunchtime because of work commitments will compare this level of service with virtually every other organisation they come into contact with, and judge the dental practice to be poor in comparison.

The quality of the product offered must be seen to be comparable with what is generally available or there is a danger of losing customers, especially if direct competiton enters the market with a better level of perceived quality.

Make it a pleasure for your customer to do business with you

Given a choice, customers will conduct business with people and organisations

Components of a dental visit	
Contacting the practice	**Going into the dental surgery**
Making an appointment	The dental chair and equipment The dentist The dental nurse The hygienist General communication with the dental team
Travelling to the practice	**Completion of the surgery visit**
Parking Entering the building Facilities for coats, etc. Facilities for children and accompanying people Dealing with pushchairs, prams etc. Finding reception inside the building Being greeted at reception	Dealing with reception for further appointments Payment How queries are dealt with at reception Recall arrangements Administration (record cards, reminder cards, etc.) Exiting the building
The waiting area	**Follow up**
Finding places in the building (the dentist's surgery, the hygienist, the toilet, the exit)	

Fig.8.4 Components of a dental visit

that they feel 'give them a fair deal'.

It is not how an organisation sees itself that is important, but how your customers perceive it. Perceptions are as individual as fingerprints. They are based on past experiences and influences — no two individuals have the same experiences so we should not be surprised when customers do not see things in the same light as the practice.

As dentistry is almost universally perceived as unpleasant, hard work is needed at improving the non-clinical aspects of each visit. Research shows that many patients seem genuinely to like their dentist but to dislike the clinical aspects of a visit. While the clinical elements of a visit can be improved by reducing discomfort and pain, patients actually expect dentistry to be slightly uncomfortable at times, as can a visit to a hospital or doctor. What they do not want is to have an unpleasant experience in the way they are treated outside the surgery itself, and this is where customer care is so important.

From time to time, go and experience things from the customer's side of the table. Phone the practice, try to do business with the practice in the same way as a patient would experience it. Impressed? If it is difficult for someone who knows the business to get what they want, think how bad it must be for a customer.

Make it easy for your customers to do business with you

This is an account of a dental patient's experience of a practice:

> *The other day I needed to make an appointment with my dentist. I tried phoning the surgery in my lunch break but all I got was an answerphone message telling me the practice was closed and who to ring in an emergency. I couldn't leave a message asking them to contact me or anything. So I slipped out from work to try and ring during the afternoon but the phone was engaged every time I tried. Finally, I asked a friend to ring for me, and when she got through she was told to hold the line for a moment and was kept waiting so long while the receptionist was sorting out appointments for someone else that she rang off. In desperation I went down the High Street during my lunch hour and found another practice that was open at lunchtime.*

Could this happen to a potential patient contacting your dental surgery? The moral of the story is; if you don't make it easy for customers to do business with you there is always a competitor that will.

Some dental examples

Dentistry is full of examples of processes, methods and systems that appear to have been created for the benefit of the practice rather than the patients.

Appointment systems are often based on what the practice wants (and often not the dentists but the receptionists). How easily can patients make appointments? Are people told when they are likely to be leaving the premises (so they can get on with the rest of their day)?

Recall systems are usually there to ensure a continued patient flow for the practice. Do recall systems enable people to obtain the type of recall and the frequency they want?

Response systems in the practice (answerphone, lunch time reception, routine correspondence, referral systems to other dentists, etc.) are usually designed for the practice.

Patient communication systems (especially for confidential matters) do not usually take the patient's feelings into account. Where are fees discussed? Who deals with difficulties in payment?

The dental surgery itself is rarely designed with the patient in mind. Almost all the surgery design caters for the dental team. While the requirements of the team must remain a high priority (after all, they spend all day in it) the patient's requirements should also be given some emphasis.

As already discussed, location of the dental practice is one of the most important factors for customers. But location means more than just the physical site. How easy is it to park in the area?(If it isn't, can the practice organise some kind of parking arrangement or pay for parking charges which may then be absorbed into the fees?). Do new patients receive a map and directions on how to reach the practice? How good is signage, especially when a new patient first enters the premises?

It is much easier to set up systems that are entirely practice-based rather than work out a system that balances patient requirements with practice needs.

The highest level of customer care?

Many people are confused when trying to determine what level of customer care they should be providing. The most difficult dilemma can often be for those people who offer different care options within their practices (i.e. NHS, private). Many seem to think that it is important to offer the highest standards of customer care at all times to all people. If we think about this logically, it does not make sense.

The level of customer care can help us to distinguish different levels of overall service to our patients. If we think about other services that we buy, very often there is a premium service for those who pay literally a premium for that service. This does not mean that the basic level of service is inferior or bad. It means that the more a customer pays, the more return the customer gets for that payment. People pay for value, or what they perceive as value, and customer care plays a large part in that equation.

From the supplier's, or practice's point of view, there are two key questions to consider. First, what is the basic level of customer care that my customers, with all of their experiences as purchasers, will accept? Second, what is the appropriate level of customer care to offer — taking into consideration all of the other aspects of the service including clinical care? It is essential that the practice staff understand this level and are able to interpret it in practical terms.

The role of staff

This brings us neatly to the fulcrum of the customer care issue. Determining policy is essential but, ironically, worthless if staff do not understand it and are not trained to implement it. Converting 'we offer the highest standards of customer care' into the practical realities of dealing with three patients at once, — all with conflicting wishes and all apparently impossible to fulfil — is key to delivering those high standards. Whilst you may not wish to train staff with a script, (indeed we would recommend quite the opposite) all members of the practice, including hygiensts and dentists must feel confident in being assertive, taking responsibility for patients as customers, communicating positive messages and helping the customer to feel positive about their experience too.

This means training. Failure to do this will result in mixed messages, a feeling of 'it's all lip service really' and ultimately bad news for the practice. Staff are the thread which brings consistency to customer care and it is consistency which determines success or failure. There is an adage which says 'that you are only as good as your last job'. Customer care is only as good as the last transaction you or your practice had with a customer. How good was that?

Conclusion

Customer care is mainly taking a different attitude — an attitude where the patient's requirements drive the practice and contribute to its success — making adjustments to services to suit patients while still keeping the practice's objectives in sight.

We all remember the people and the places that have put effort into customer care. If we want to remain competitive — we must offer the same to our own customers.

Afterword

Many of the marketing concepts contained within this book can be difficult to grasp initially, and at this stage, the reader may still be 'slightly uncertain'. However, let us focus again on the purpose of this book. It is about helping dentists and those who work within dental practice to understand what marketing is and how to apply it in an ethical and professional way for three reasons.
These are:

- To make your dental practice or organisation as effective a business as possible
- To make your professional working life as enjoyable and fulfilling as possible
- To provide a means of educating and raising the awareness of the benefits and advantages of dentistry to the population at large.

Good marketing and robust marketing systems can achieve all of these things, but as we have seen, it is a complex, constant and cohesive process. Marketing is relevant to any practice, new or old, NHS or private, busy or not. It is not just about having the right brochure, putting in an advertisement or running a patient questionnaire. It is about planning, having clear objectives, and willingness. It can be hard work. However, for those willing to do what is required, the results will almost certainly be greater than you may imagine.

Index

Index

Index